LSD

Mary Ann Littell

—The Drug Library—

Enslow Publishers, Inc.

44 Fadem Road	PO Box 38
Box 699	Aldershot
Springfield, NJ 07081	Hants GU12 6BP
USA	UK

Library of Congress Cataloging-in-Publication Data

Littell, Mary Ann.
    LSD / Mary Ann Littell.
       p. cm. — (The Drug library)
    Includes bibliographical references and index.
    Summary: Looks at the history of the hallucinogenic drug
LSD and its societal and physical effects.
    ISBN 0-89490-739-5
    1. LSD (Drug)—United States—Juvenile literature. 2. Hallucinogenic
drugs—United States—Case studies—Juvenile literature. 3. Drug abuse—
United States—Prevention—Juvenile literature. [1. LSD (Drug)
2. Hallucinogenic drugs. 3. Drugs. 4. Drug Abuse.] I. Title. II. Series.
HV5822.L9L57 1996
362.29'4—dc20   96-6864
                                          CIP
                                          AC

Printed in the United States of America

10 9 8 7 6 5 4 3 2

Photo Credits: D.A.R.E., p. 90; DEA, pp. 7, 23, 25, 38, 47, 72; Enslow
Publishers Inc., p. 14; Mary Ann Littell, p. 43; Partnership for a Drug-Free
America, p. 58.

Cover Photo: DEA

Contents

1 The History of LSD   5

2 LSD and Its Effects 19

3 LSD: Then and Now 34

4 The Faces Behind LSD Abuse 50

5 LSD and Families 65

6 Treatment, Recovery,
   and Prevention 79

   Where to Go for Help 94

   Chapter Notes 97

   Glossary 106

   Further Reading 109

   Index 111

1

The History of LSD

LSD, or lysergic acid diethylamide, is the most well known of the hallucinogenic class of drugs. Hallucinogens, also known as psychedelics, are a group of drugs that affect the central nervous system. These drugs change the way a person sees reality. Some hallucinogens are artificially made, while others grow naturally. LSD is artificial. It is made from lysergic acid, which is why the drug is often called "acid." Lysergic acid is found in ergot, a fungus that grows on rye, wheat, and other grains. It can also be made from lysergic acid amide.

The Discovery of LSD

While many well-known drugs have been around for generations, LSD is relatively new on the drug scene. It was discovered by Dr. Albert Hofmann, a Swiss chemist working for Sandoz

Pharmaceutical, a chemical company. Hofmann was doing research to find new medications to relieve headache pain. He was working with the ergot fungus, which was thought to contain many medicinal chemicals.

In 1938, while working in his laboratory, Hofmann synthesized, or made, a new chemical. He called his discovery lysergic acid diethylamide, or LSD. Scientists performed some tests with the new chemical, but did not find any uses for it. So the LSD was put aside.

In 1943, Hofmann again began to test the drug he had discovered five years earlier. On April 16, while handling LSD without gloves, he accidentally ingested, or swallowed, a tiny amount of the drug. He immediately began feeling strange and confused, almost like being drunk. He left work and went home to lie down.

Hofmann suspected that LSD was responsible for his strange sensations, but he was not sure. He could not believe LSD was such a potent substance. Later that week, Hofmann deliberately took another, larger dose of LSD. He felt the same strange sensations he had before. Only this time, they were more intense and lasted longer.[1]

LSD in Early Times

As the discoverer of LSD, Hofmann was most likely the first modern-day scientist to experience an LSD "trip." However, the powerful effects of the drug had actually been felt hundreds of years earlier. In medieval times, many communities baked bread from rye and wheat flour. Sometimes this flour was contaminated with the ergot fungus. Ergot appears on grains as a purple or rust-colored substance. It can be difficult to see. After eating

LSD is manufactured at "acid labs" like this one. Making the drug is illegal, so the manufacturers work in secret. They set up temporary labs in out-of-the-way neighborhoods or remote areas of the countryside. After making the drug, they remove their equipment and leave the area.

ergot-contaminated bread, entire towns of people would become ill with a disease called St. Anthony's fire. Their symptoms included dizziness, hallucinations (seeing, hearing, or feeling things that are not real), convulsions, and even gangrene, the blackening and death of the body's soft tissues. When the sick traveled to a shrine to pray for recovery, their symptoms disappeared— probably because they were no longer eating the bread that had made them ill in the first place.[2]

The people of these medieval towns did not know the cause of their hallucinations. However, other ancient people knowingly used mind-altering substances during religious ceremonies and special events. These were not drugs as we know them, but plants, leaves, and seeds that grew in nature. They were chewed, eaten, or made into potions.

The Aztecs chewed peyote and other substances, including morning glory seeds, which contained lysergic acid. Australian Aborigines chewed pituri, a small shrub growing wild in the desert. Many Spanish cultures chewed peyote and coca leaves. Some ancient Native American and Mexican communities ate mushrooms that were thought to contain mystical properties.

Early people believed these plants were medicines with mystical healing properties. Usually, religious leaders of groups or tribes were the ones who knew about these primitive medicines. These "medicine men and women" controlled the use of the medicines, and therefore had a great deal of power. They passed along their knowledge from generation to generation. The medicines were not used frequently. They were saved for special occasions, usually religious rituals and ceremonies.

With the growth of Christianity, people changed their beliefs and religious practices. As Christianity spread, people began to cut back on the use of mind-altering substances. They connected the use of these types of plants with witchcraft and worship of the devil. These medicines were found to be dangerous, and were therefore outlawed.[3]

LSD: A New Wonder Drug?

After Dr. Hofmann accidentally took LSD, he wrote extensively about his experiences with it. News of the drug spread quickly. Many scientists and doctors thought it could be a wonder drug, effective in curing all types of mental illnesses.[4] First, however, LSD would have to be tested to be sure it was safe and effective.

The Food, Drug, and Cosmetic Act of 1938 stated that before a drug could be sold, it had to be tested on both animals and humans. In 1953, Sandoz Pharmaceuticals received permission from the Food and Drug Administration (FDA) to test LSD in the United States. The FDA allowed Sandoz to distribute LSD only to qualified psychiatrists and only for research purposes.

Over the next ten years, researchers in the United States performed experiments with LSD. Medical doctors and psychologists at major universities conducted most of the tests. The drug was used to treat many problems, from mental illness to alcoholism. Some early research was conducted at Emory University on prisoners from the Atlanta prison. Many of them experienced "bad trips," or frightening hallucinations, and reacted by screaming and hiding under tables. It was very frightening. By the early 1960s, more than two thousand articles and studies about the new "miracle drug" appeared in medical journals around the world.[5]

The Central Intelligence Agency (CIA) and the United States Army also tested the new drug to learn if it could be used in chemical warfare. Chemical warfare is the use of drugs and chemical substances as weapons of war. In the 1950s, Americans feared that Communist countries, particularly Russia, might develop a chemical weapon that could be used to brainwash entire nations. So the CIA and the army began research to find their own chemical weapons. One top-secret program, named MKUltra, did studies on LSD and other psychedelic drugs to see if they could be used for brainwashing or mind control.[6]

The CIA's experiments were done secretly. People involved in the testing later said they were given LSD without being told what it was. Many who took part in the experiments became ill and never recovered. The CIA and the army did not admit to testing people without their consent. However, some of the victims and their families have sued and received money as a settlement. The family of Harold Blauer, a tennis professional who died shortly after participating in an army experiment more than forty years ago, sued the CIA. A court awarded the family $700,000 in damages.[7]

From the Labs to the Streets

The results of ten years of LSD testing were a disaster. The drug was so unpredictable that its effectiveness could not be measured. It was impossible to tell if LSD was a safe drug. Doctors could not find proof that it helped cure any kind of illness. There were many unanswered questions about possible harmful side effects. It was beginning to look as though LSD was not safe at all.

However, experimentation with the drug continued—in the laboratories and out of them as well. As word of LSD's powerful effects spread, there was a great deal of curiosity about the drug. At the universities where LSD was being tested, many students were eager to try acid. Although most researchers were ethical, or honest, and obeyed the drug testing laws, a few broke the laws. They began taking the drug themselves, even though they were not supposed to. They also gave the drug to people outside the research setting.

The United States government, concerned about the increasing abuse of LSD and other drugs, passed new drug-testing laws in 1963. These new laws said that research had to be done in a safe and scientific manner. In 1965, other new laws made it a crime to sell or distribute LSD. The purpose of these laws was to be sure that LSD was tested carefully and used only for research purposes. Unfortunately, even though the new laws were very strict, illegal use of LSD continued.

As more and more people heard about LSD, and tried it, demand for the drug grew. As a result, LSD became widely available on the "black market." It was for sale illegally in cities and on college campuses across the country. The Sixties was a time of rising drug use and abuse. The chart on the following page shows the different hallucinogenic drugs available at this time.

The Drug Abuse Control Amendments of 1965 made it illegal to sell, give away, or distribute LSD or any other drug "having the potential for abuse."[8] All researchers were required to turn over their supplies of LSD to the FDA. This way, the government could try to control the use of LSD. By 1966, most states had passed laws against the possession of LSD. In 1968, the government revised existing laws and banned use of the drug altogether.

These new laws decreased the supply of available LSD, but did not completely eliminate it. Too much of the drug was already in circulation. Too many researchers and chemists knew how to make it.

In 1970, LSD and all other psychedelic drugs were placed into the Schedule I category of the Controlled Substances Act. This classification was for frequently abused drugs with no medical use. Most research on LSD abruptly stopped. By now, however, the damage had been done. LSD was now the drug of choice for many drug abusers on the streets.

Types of Hallucinogens

Naturally Occuring	Artificially Occuring
Belladonna	LSD (lysergic acid diethylamide)
Hen Bane	Mescaline
Jimson Weed	Psilocybin
Mandrake	DMT (dimethyltryptamine)
Marijuana	Ketamine
Nightshade	MDA (methylenedioxyamphetamine)
Peyote	PCP (phencyclidine)
Morning Glory Seeds (certain varieties)	TMA (trimethyloxyamphetamine)
Mushrooms (certain varieties)	

Trends in LSD Use

LSD use was at its worst in the early 1960s, with millions of young Americans trying the drug. Use did drop sharply in the late 1960s and early 1970s, when the ban on LSD made it harder to buy and sell. From May 1966 through March 1967, drug agents seized over 1.5 million doses of hallucinogens, mostly LSD. The street value of these drugs was approximately $9 million.[9]

A better understanding of the dangers of LSD and negative

publicity about "bad trips" were the main reasons for the decline in LSD use. The acid of the 1960s was a strong and powerful drug. It was also very unpredictable. Because the drug changed a user's perception of reality, people who were high on LSD did strange things. People on "bad trips"—jumping out of windows and in front of moving cars—all appeared in newspapers and on the evening news. Many people were made aware of the risks and stopped using acid. It was just too dangerous.

About 10 million Americans have tried LSD at least once, according to the National Institute on Drug Abuse. And even though acid fell out of favor in the late 1960s, its use is once again on the rise. In a 1990 survey, 8.7 percent of high school seniors said they had used acid.[10] Three years later, 10.3 percent of high school seniors reported using acid, according to another study.[11] Although this is only a slight increase, it indicates a trend toward more LSD use. A whole new generation of LSD users who were not around in the 1960s may now believe that the drug is a safe alternative to cocaine or marijuana. It is not, and never has been.

Even more alarming is the fact that the number of students who think LSD is dangerous has declined. In a recent survey, only 38.3 percent of eighth graders said that they thought taking LSD once or twice was harmful. Many researchers believe that drug use is influenced by how dangerous a drug is believed to be. Therefore, the perception that LSD is not harmful may lead to its increased use.[12]

The federal government, concerned about the increased use of LSD, has gotten tough on lawbreakers. In 1993, Drug Enforcement Agency (DEA) drug busts seized four times as many psychedelic drugs as were seized in 1990.[13]

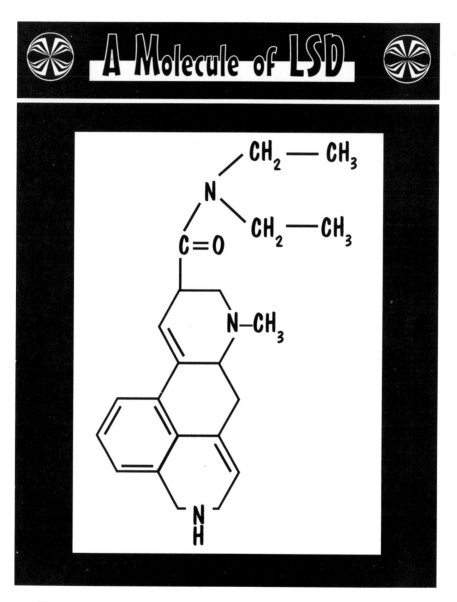

This is what a molecule of LSD looks like. LSD, or lysergic acid diethylamide, is a chemical compound. It is made from ergot, a fungus which grows on wheat and other grains.

After all these years, why is LSD popular once again? Partly because this new generation of users does not know much about its negative effects. Most schools offer drug and alcohol education. However, specific information about LSD is rarely included in antidrug programs today.

Americans who were young adults in the 1960s remember the dangers of LSD. Whether or not they used the drug, they heard many stories about bad trips, including frightening hallucinations and flashbacks. The current generation sees LSD much differently. They were not around during the Sixties, so they may not have heard the terrifying stories about LSD use that were so common back then. They know more about the harmful effects of crack and cocaine, because these drugs are often in the news. But they probably do not know much about LSD. To them, it may seem less dangerous than other substances. It is, however, quite dangerous.

The LSD Mystique—Then and Now

LSD has always been a drug used mostly by white, middle-class people, especially males under the age of twenty. In the Sixties, it was popular on college campuses. Dr. Timothy Leary, a former Harvard psychologist and one of the first LSD researchers, coined the phrase, "Turn on, tune in, drop out," to describe the LSD trip.

In the Sixties, LSD had strong ties to rock music and concerts. The Beatles and other rock groups openly discussed taking LSD and other drugs.[14] The connection between rock music and LSD remains strong. Many drug users consider hallucinogens, and particularly LSD, a "must" at rock concerts. In 1994, undercover police officers arrested 173 people for possession or sale of LSD, marijuana, and cocaine during a single weekend of Grateful Dead concerts in Phoenix, Arizona.[15]

Despite the similarities, there is one important difference between today's LSD and the acid of the Sixties—the strength of the drug. Back in the Sixties, a typical dose of LSD was 150 to 300 micrograms. (A microgram is one millionth of a gram.) Today's dose, 20 to 80 micrograms, is much weaker. Therefore, users may take more of the drug to get high. With LSD, as with alcohol and other drugs, the more you take, the stronger the effects will be. This leads to increasingly dangerous behavior.

Many users who want an intense high "piggyback" the drug, taking several doses at a time. LSD can lead users to do dangerous things. In Fairfax County, Virginia, in 1991, a high-school student high on acid shot and seriously wounded a police officer.[16] In 1994, a nineteen-year-old boy from Hagaman, New York, shot his mother while she slept, then turned the gun on himself. State police believe the teenager was tripping on LSD when he committed the crimes.[17]

LSD's unpredictability has tragic results. One drug counselor said, "If you give a youngster three beers, you have a good idea how they're going to behave. You take the same kid and give him a hit of acid and you don't know what's going to happen."[18]

Unpredictability is not the only hazard of LSD. It can also harm a user's health. Doctors are particularly concerned about use among younger adolescents. "The younger you are," said David Smith, M.D., "the more likely you are to impair your psychosocial development and have adverse reactions."[19]

"Younger children, at eighth-grade level and below, are at greater risk," says researcher Larry Chait, "because their personalities haven't developed well enough to know how to handle altered states of consciousness. As with any drug, the younger the age of first use, the higher the risk."[20] However, LSD is dangerous for anyone, at any age.

The United States government estimates that people in this country spend about $40 billion to $50 billion a year on illegal drugs. But the estimated total expense of drug abuse is far higher. The problem of alcohol and other drug abuse costs an additional $143 billion per year in this country. Total dollar amounts include the price of hospital stays, property damage (due to drug-induced episodes), time lost from work, and law enforcement attempts. Learning the facts about LSD might help you or someone you know to stay clean.

Questions for Discussion

1. Why do you think many drug education programs fail to address the dangers of LSD?

2. What are some reasons you can think of to explain the recent rise in LSD use?

3. Production of LSD is widespread even though it is illegal. Can you think of any methods that could be used to curb the making of LSD?

2

LSD and Its Effects

During the 1960s, San Francisco was famous as a center for drugs, particularly LSD and other hallucinogens. Today, most of the LSD sold in the United States and Canada is made in San Francisco.[1] Smaller amounts of the drug are produced in other northwestern cities. Large quantities are also made in the Netherlands.

Where Does LSD Come From?

A handful of drug makers, perhaps ten or twelve in all, make enough uncut LSD to supply the entire world.[2] Uncut LSD is still in chemical form. It must be processed before it can be used.

San Francisco is the main distribution point for the drug. From there, mail and package delivery services unknowingly ship quantities of uncut LSD all over the world, to people who process and sell it.

Manufacturing LSD is against the law. To avoid being arrested, the makers of the drug are very secretive. They operate small "acid labs" in out-of-the-way sections of a city, or rent motel rooms to use as temporary laboratories. Other manufacturers have rented small farms in the countryside, setting up their labs in barns. After a few weeks or months, they move to another location, carrying their equipment in suitcases or pickup trucks.[3] Laboratory operators often carry guns. Weapons and explosives are frequently seized when police raid LSD labs, making law enforcement's job both difficult and dangerous.

How the Drug Is Made

LSD is first made into crystals. This process takes up to one week, and must be done with care to avoid accidentally ingesting the chemical.[4]

Crystal LSD can be combined with alcohol to form a liquid. The drug is shipped in either crystal or liquid form to people who process and sell it.

Different Forms of LSD

LSD is available in several different forms. The chart on the following page illustrates the most common ones.

One form of LSD that is *not* available—and never has been—is the sticker. A few years ago, there were rumors of a new LSD sticker that would stick to the skin and make the wearer high. These stickers were said to be targeted to young children at playgrounds and school yards. It was also rumored that the

Forms of LSD

Name	Form
MICRODOTS	Tablets that are swallowed like pills. They are so tiny that it would take at least ten of them to equal the size of an aspirin tablet.
WINDOWPANE	Small, thin sheets of gelatin cut into tiny squares.
SUGAR CUBES	Cubes of sugar, saturated with liquid LSD.
BLOTTER PAPER	Sheets of absorbent paper soaked in LSD solution and dried. The paper is decorated with rows of cartoon characters, zodiac signs, or other illustrations, then perforated like a sheet of postage stamps. Users tear off one- to two-centimeter squares of the paper and lick or chew it.
EYE DROPS	Liquid LSD is added to a bottle of eye drops. Users place drops into their eyes.

stickers were decorated with pictures of Disney characters and other figures appealing to children.

The rumors frightened parents and school officials across the country. However, there was no reason for concern. The stickers did not exist. Drug experts say that it would be practically impossible to get high while wearing an LSD sticker. Since LSD is not easily absorbed through the skin, a sticker could not hold enough LSD to get a wearer high.

How LSD Is Taken

Because LSD is not smoked, injected, or sniffed, many users assume it is a safe drug, not nearly as dangerous as crack, heroin, or cocaine. However, the way a drug is taken does not necessarily determine whether it is a dangerous or safe substance. LSD is a very dangerous substance for anyone who takes it, and in any form. Some scientists believe that the drug can even cause birth defects in the babies of women who take LSD during pregnancy. LSD users can become tolerant of the drug very quickly. After three or four days of use, it loses its effect and a user will no longer be able to get high. He or she will have to either stop taking the drug for several days or even a few weeks before trying it again, or increase the amount of LSD taken.

Because LSD produces tolerance, regular users eventually have to take more and more of it to get high. Some take repeated doses of the drug. Other LSD users look for more creative ways to enhance the LSD high. A resident of a rehabilitation program reported placing sheets of dissolvable LSD behind her eyelids so it would reach her brain more quickly.[5] In an effort to enhance their LSD high, users can do some very dangerous things.

Making LSD requires some knowledge of chemistry. The drug is first made into crystals, then combined with alcohol to form a liquid. Care must be taken to avoid accidentally ingesting the drug.

Is Acid Addictive?

LSD does not produce the same physical craving as other addictive drugs, such as heroin. However, regular acid users can become psychologically dependent on LSD. They prefer the feeling of being high on the drug than being without it.

A typical dose of LSD in the Sixties was many times stronger than today's average dose. Back then, it was not unusual to take 300 micrograms of acid or more. In the Sixties, an LSD high was often referred to as a "trip." Sometimes other travel words, like "journey" or "tour," were used to describe the LSD experience. Of course, the user did not physically go anywhere. The trip was strictly in the mind. Why did people use travel metaphors when talking about LSD? Probably because the drug had such a dramatic effect on the user's mind.

Since LSD is a street drug, there is no way of knowing how strong a dose really is. Perhaps the chemist who made the drug added too much LSD to the mixture. Or maybe the blotter paper used was extra-absorbent, and soaked up more of the drug. When someone buys LSD on the street, at a concert, or from a friend, they know they are getting a powerful drug. But they do not know just how powerful. Because of this, today's LSD has the potential to be as dangerous as the drug of the Sixties.

Metabolizing LSD

While LSD is available in many forms, by far the most commonly used type is blotter paper. A user chews or swallows the paper to ingest the acid. The drug then goes through the normal digestive process. It is absorbed from the body's gastrointestinal

Blotter paper, pictured above, is the most common form of LSD. Sheets of absorbent paper are soaked in liquid LSD and dried. The paper is decorated with cartoon characters, zodiac signs, or other illustrations, and perforated like a sheet of postage stamps. Each square of paper is a single dose of LSD.

tract (the part of the body that digests foods) and mucous membranes (the linings of body passages and cavities).

LSD is absorbed rapidly by most body tissues, particularly the kidneys and liver. Only very small amounts actually travel through the bloodstream to the brain. However, that is enough to make a user feel high. As little as a single microgram of the drug has an effect on the body. Fifty micrograms are enough to produce intense sensations.

Levels of LSD in the body are highest about one hour after taking the drug.[6] The typical LSD trip is at its peak a few hours after the drug is taken. A trip lasts about six to eight hours before the effects gradually begin to wear off.[7]

Researchers are not sure exactly how LSD works on the human brain. They think the drug affects the body's neurotransmitters. These are chemicals in the body that help nerve cells communicate. The basic unit of the body's central nervous system is the nerve cell, or neuron. Chains of nerve cells transmit impulses, or messages, from the brain throughout the body. The neurotransmitters help the impulses move from cell to cell. LSD's chemical structure is similar to many of these neurotransmitters. Therefore, scientists believe that LSD and other hallucinogens influence the messages that pass among the body's neurotransmitters.[8] LSD affects the body in many ways, including:

- *elevated body temperature and blood pressure*
- *increased heart rate*
- *increased perspiration*
- *dilated pupils*
- *reduced muscle control and coordination*
- *dizziness, weakness, and numbness*

- *headaches and heart palpitations (a feeling that the heart is pounding)*
- *shortness of breath*
- *nausea and vomiting*

Not everyone experiences all these body changes every time. LSD is unpredictable, so there is no way to determine what the effects will be, or how long a trip will last. Everyone who takes the drug has a different reaction to it. A user may experience a good trip or a bad trip.

Bad trips are very unpleasant, even frightening experiences. Someone on a bad trip frequently loses all sense of reality and behaves in bizarre and dangerous ways. In 1994, in Antelope Valley, California, a teenager who had taken LSD with friends tried to break into a neighbor's home in the middle of the night. The frightened homeowner called 911 and warned the teen to stop, then shot him twice in the upper body. Not even two bullet wounds could stop the drug-crazed teen. Despite his injuries, he dove through a window into the house, nearly severing his leg on broken glass. The homeowner fought him until the police finally arrived. The teenager later died of multiple injuries.[9]

LSD and the Mind

LSD affects a person's mind in two ways: through sensory and emotional changes.

Sensory changes. The effects of LSD on a person's senses are often called psychedelic, meaning mind-altering. The drug changes the way a person sees reality. Ordinary shapes and objects are distorted, or look different than they really are.

Inanimate things, things that do not move, may seem to move unexpectedly. Sound is distorted, and judgment of time and space is affected. People on LSD often claim they can hear colors and see sounds. This mixing of the senses is called synesthesia.[10]

Emotional changes. Feelings and moods become more intense and changeable. The user may feel very emotional, often laughing or crying uncontrollably. Sometimes it becomes more difficult to communicate with others.

Some people think a person's mood determines what type of trip he or she will have. They believe that unhappy people are more likely to have bad trips, while happy, upbeat people will have good trips. This perception is one of the most common and persistent myths about LSD. While state of mind can affect an LSD trip, it does not determine whether a trip will be good or bad. A good mood does not guarantee a good trip. There is simply no way to predict a user's experience. Furthermore, having had good LSD trips in the past does not guarantee good trips in the future. The effects of LSD are very unpredictable, and quite dangerous.

A bad trip can happen at any time, to any LSD user. However, the stronger the dose, the more likely a person is to have a bad trip. With continued use, LSD users are more likely to take larger doses to get high. Therefore, they may be most prone to having bad trips.

During a bad trip, the user feels anxious, depressed, and panicky. Often, he or she is confused and disoriented. The room may appear to be spinning. Most overwhelming is the sense of being totally out of control. Users may do things that are harmful to themselves or others while on a bad trip. Other negative effects of a bad LSD trip are:

Paranoia or suspicion. Fearing others are out to harm them.

Distorted images. Ordinary objects take on a different appearance: People may look like monsters or animals.

The "Superman" syndrome. People high on LSD often think they are indestructible and they may behave bizarrely. LSD users have been known to run onto busy highways, jump out windows, and do other dangerous things.

Intense unhappiness or depression. Often accompanied by mood swings: happy one minute, sad the next.

Hallucinations. Users see, hear, or feel things that are not real. While most users know their hallucinations are not real, others cannot tell the difference between illusion and reality.

Flashbacks. Even after a bad trip is over, users can reexperience some of its effects days, weeks, months, or even years later. Flashbacks may recur even if the user has not taken another dose of LSD. People who have flashbacks see many of the psychedelic images they saw while being high on the drug.

Many people think that if they take LSD in a calm, peaceful environment, among friends, they will be sure to have a good trip. This is yet another myth. There is no guarantee that taking the drug in pleasant surroundings will result in a good trip.

Out of Control

Sometimes a reaction to LSD is so severe that a user totally loses touch with the real world. In the early stages of a bad trip, the psychedelic effects may become so frightening that the user panics. In the later stages, the user may become psychotic. Psychosis is a total loss of contact with reality. It is similar to a state of temporary insanity. At this point, the user may be a danger to himself or herself, or to others. In these cases, medical help is needed. Other dangerous symptoms include:

- *extreme depression (often occurs up to twenty-four hours following LSD use)*
- *attempts at suicide*
- *violent behavior (toward self or others)*
- *recurring hallucinations or flashbacks*

It is very difficult to die from an overdose of LSD. However, LSD does impair a user's judgment and good sense. People do dangerous things while on the drug. Sometimes, this behavior leads to serious injury or even death. Drownings, burns, falls, auto accidents, and even suicide have been the tragic consequences of LSD use. Back in the 1950s, a mentally ill patient at a Massachusetts clinic committed suicide hours after taking LSD. She was given LSD without her knowledge, as part of an experiment to study its effects. The drug was given to her after she had recovered from her illness and was ready to go home.[11]

Today's LSD can still lead to dangerous behavior. One resident of a drug rehabilitation program described hitting her sister on the head with a beer bottle while tripping. "Acid can affect you for the rest of your life," she said.[12]

LSD users on bad trips may be so out of touch with reality that they do not realize they need medical help. They are usually brought to hospital emergency rooms by the police or by friends who are alarmed by their behavior.

The Drug Abuse Warning Network (DAWN) gathers statistics on how many drug users visit hospital emergency rooms for medical treatment each year. While emergency-room visits for cocaine and other drugs decreased between 1985 and 1990, LSD visits increased by 65 percent. Half of these visits were for young people between the ages of ten and nineteen.[13] In 1991, hallucinogen use resulted in more than eight thousand visits to emergency rooms.[14]

Long-Term Health Risks

A typical bad trip will usually wear off in several hours. Some bad trips, however, can last for days, weeks, or even months. In the worst cases, users may need to be hospitalized and treated with tranquilizers.

LSD users, particularly those who used the drug heavily, suffer permanent damage. This damage is mental, rather than physical. It includes permanent personality changes, chronic depression, flashbacks, confusion, and other unpleasant symptoms. Who will be part of that unlucky group? It is impossible to predict.

Brian Wilson, the musical genius behind the Beach Boys, a popular 1960s group, remembered taking one bad acid trip that changed his life forever. "It screwed my mind up on me," he said, adding that he wished he had never taken it. The drug affected his mental health and songwriting abilities and put his career on hold for many years.[15]

Victims of LSD will never be the same as they were before they took the drug. Some are described as having "fried brains." They will need ongoing medical treatment, including psychiatric care, even after they have kicked the habit. Many of them may never be able to hold a job or live a normal life. A single trip can result in long-term problems.

LSD and the Environment

Acid is not just harmful to individuals. It is a serious hazard to the environment as well, though many people do not know it. The manufacture of LSD and other illegal drugs pollutes our land and our water.

All manufacturers must obey certain laws when disposing of chemical wastes and other dangerous or polluting substances. These laws were designed to protect the environment. Unfortunately, most illegal drug manufacturers do not care about these laws or the environment. They are mainly concerned with making a profit and avoiding arrest. According to the Drug Enforcement Agency (DEA), manufacturers of LSD and other illegal drugs have dumped toxic chemical by-products on the ground, in lakes and streams, and even in local sewage systems. By-products are the chemicals that are left over after a substance is manufactured. The result is pollution of land and water costing millions of dollars in cleanups.

One drug maker set up a laboratory on rented farmland in the Northeast. During the manufacturing process, chemicals were dumped all over the property. After the drug makers left, the owners discovered that their farmland and well had been poisoned by the discarded chemicals. The federal government had to hire commercial contractors to clean up the site of the abandoned drug lab. The cleanup cost more than $3 million.[16]

LSD use affects all of us—even those who have never used the drug. As a result, the DEA has stepped up its efforts to get the drug—and the drug makers—out of circulation.

Questions for Discussion

1. What actions would indicate someone has taken LSD? What would you do if your friend took LSD and had a bad trip?

2. The effects of LSD are unpredictable and dangerous. What are some of the effects LSD can have on a user? In turn, what are some of the effects the user can have on others?

3. The manufacture of LSD pollutes our land and water. Can you suggest some ways to help prevent the pollution of the environment by illegal LSD labs?

3

LSD: Then and Now

LSD first came on the scene in the 1960s, a time of great social change in America. Many people believe that this is when America's drug problem truly began. It actually started long before that, even before the turn of the century.

Roots of Drug Addiction

LSD is a psychoactive drug. Psychoactive drugs influence or change the way the mind works. They affect moods, emotions, feelings, and thoughts. Some psychoactive drugs, such as heroin, codeine, morphine, cocaine, and opium, are narcotics. Narcotics dull the feeling of pain and produce a strong high. They are extremely addictive. Narcotics have long been prescribed by doctors to treat people who are in pain. Many narcotics are ingredients in prescription medicines still in use today.

The use of psychoactive drugs dates back to the late 1800s. Back then, many strong narcotic drugs, including opium, cocaine, and morphine, could be bought right at the corner drugstore without a prescription. These drugs were the main ingredients in patent medicines—medicines that were used to treat headaches, stomach ailments, toothaches, nervousness, and practically every other known illness. Patent medicines promised to cure menstrual cramps and other "female problems," and even colic (gas) and teething pain in babies. Today it is hard to imagine giving such strong drugs to infants. Back then, it was accepted.

At the turn of the century, patent medicines were big business. Their manufacturers spent thousands of dollars advertising in newspapers and magazines. Medicine shows toured around the country to spread the word about these "miracle tonics." Even though patent medicines contained strong drugs, they were not considered dangerous. Many people took them regularly to relieve their aches and pains. Without realizing it, they became addicted, or physically dependent, on these medicines.

Patent medicines were not the only drugs on the market. Stronger medicines containing narcotics were also available by prescription. Doctors regularly gave these medications to their patients to relieve pain, decrease anxiety, and ease other chronic symptoms that would not go away. Many patients became hooked on these powerful medicines.

The result of all this drug-taking was widespread addiction. In 1900, there were more drug addicts in America, in proportion to the population, than there are today. By the 1920s, an estimated half a million people were hooked on narcotics.[1] These users were called medical addicts because they were addicted to prescription medicines.

Early Attitudes

Before the 1900s, drug addiction was not considered as negatively as it is now. Many people considered addiction simply an unfortunate result of taking medications. The medicines were not illegal, so how harmful could they be? Millions of readers followed the adventures of the famous fictional detective, Sherlock Holmes, without objecting to his cocaine addiction.[2]

However, as time progressed, the number of addicts grew at an alarming rate. Government officials became concerned. By the early 1900s, attitudes had changed. It was no longer all right to be dependent on strong medicines. Newspaper and magazine articles criticized patent medicine makers for turning America into a nation of addicts.

In 1906, the government passed the Pure Food and Drug Act, which required drug manufacturers to list any drugs that were in their medicines. In 1914, the Harrison Act was passed, making it against the law to get narcotic drugs without prescriptions. During the 1920s, other laws made it illegal for doctors to continue prescribing narcotics to addicted patients.

The new antidrug laws seemed to work. The use of drugs dropped dramatically. By 1945, the number of addicts had declined to between forty and fifty thousand.[3] Since selling narcotic drugs was now against the law, these users obtained their drugs on the black market.

"Turn on, tune in, drop out"

While medical addiction was common in the first half of the twentieth century, recreational drug use—using drugs to get high—was not widespread.

During the 1960s, however, there were many changes in people's behavior and attitudes. The Sixties has been idealized as a time of personal freedom, adventure, and "doing your own thing." Being an individual was more important than conforming. Many young people became involved with social activism by protesting against the injustices of society. They rebelled against authority—their parents, the police, and even the government. Experimenting with drugs was part of this rebellion.

The rebellion was fueled by America's involvement in an unpopular war in Vietnam, a small country in Southeast Asia. Young people protested against this war. At the time, young men could be drafted, or made to serve in the military. Many young people were against the draft—particularly for a war they did not believe in.

People who grew up in the 1960s are often called the Woodstock Generation, after the famous rock music festival. Rock music was an important part of the Sixties, and there was a strong connection between music and drugs. Young people "tuned in" to the loud music, "turned on" to drugs, and "dropped out" of conventional society into their own way of life. Many of them were "turning on" with LSD.

By the mid-Sixties, LSD use was at its worst. In a survey of eighteen- to twenty-five-year-olds, more than 30 percent said they had tried LSD at least once.[4] The drug had almost become a fad—the "in" thing among drug users.

Reports of LSD-related injuries and even deaths appeared in newspapers and on the evening news. One doctor claimed that a group of students "tripping" on LSD looked into the sun and went blind.[5] Other reports blamed the drug for genetic and brain damage.[6] These accounts were enough to frighten people away

Vials of liquid LSD like those pictured here are shipped all over the world. Only a small amount of liquid LSD is needed to make many doses of the drug.

from taking LSD. As with most fads, the public eventually lost interest in LSD.

Stiff laws against LSD also contributed to its decline. Federal laws passed in the late 1960s made manufacture of the drug a serious crime. Other state laws made it a crime to possess or buy LSD. The sentences for LSD are much more severe than those for other drugs. One gram of LSD produces about twenty thousand doses. By law, the extra weight of the paper, sugar, or water combined with the LSD must be added to the weight of the drug when calculating a prison sentence. So someone with a small amount of LSD stored on as few as five sugar cubes could go to prison for years.[7] Many people decided that dealing acid was not worth the risk.

In the 1970s and 1980s, antidrug campaigns taught an awareness of drug abuse. By the early 1980s, abuse of all drugs, including LSD, decreased. In 1985, LSD abuse was at an all-time low. However, abuse of two other drugs was on the rise: crack and cocaine. Since LSD seemed to be a thing of the past, it was dropped from many antidrug education programs. Instead, attention was focused on cocaine and crack. Cocaine received even more bad publicity when it was linked to the death of famous athletes, including basketball star Len Bias.

Many experts believe that actual use of LSD and other drugs is probably even higher than reported. Most drug abusers do not spend much time in high school. They either drop out or have poor attendance. Consequently, students with the worst drug problems are not counted in high school surveys.[8]

Researchers, law enforcers, and doctors are concerned about the recent rise in LSD abuse. LSD was one of the first drugs to become popular during the drug epidemic of the 1960s. It was also the first drug to fall out of favor. Does its return indicate the beginning of a new epidemic? Only time will tell.

The increase in LSD abuse seems to reflect generational forgetting. Such forgetting occurs when a new generation does not get the same chance as the previous generation to learn important messages. "The need for leadership and broad participation in drug prevention is not just for a year or two, but rather for the next decade and beyond. The national commitment to drug-free youth must be long-term. Our nation's children deserve no less."[9]

Patterns of Drug Use Today

Drug use remains widespread among young people. Many begin by drinking alcohol, sometimes as early as the elementary school years. Some students progress to other drugs, such as marijuana, LSD, and amphetamines, by the time they reach middle school. Drug abuse seems to reach its peak by twelfth grade overall, but can still continue through the college years.

Even though many young people continue to experiment with drugs during their school years, overall use of some illegal drugs declined during the past decade. However, in 1993, the use of marijuana and other illegal drugs began to rise again. The consumption of "gateway drugs"—marijuana, tobacco, and alcohol—continues to rise.[10]

It is inaccurate, however, to lump all these drugs together. Alcohol and tobacco are not illegal, and it is socially acceptable for adults to use them. Many adults make the decision to drink and smoke, even though studies have shown alcohol and tobacco to be serious health hazards. Society disapproves of young people drinking and smoking, and there are laws against selling tobacco and alcohol to minors. All states prohibit the use of alcohol and tobacco by young people. However, most teens do not see the harm in drinking and smoking. Many do not even consider alcohol to be a drug.

On the other hand, the use of illegal substances is unacceptable for any group, regardless of age. Such drugs have no legitimate place in our society.

A Pill for Everything

Even though patent medicines are a thing of the past, many Americans still largely rely on medications to make them feel better. They take pills for headaches, stomachaches, sore throats, and a variety of other ailments. Hundreds of different vitamin supplements promise to keep their bodies strong. There are medicines for indigestion, constipation, diarrhea, and even weight loss. For every physical problem, there is supposed to be a cure in the form of a pill.

People take medications for emotional as well as physical ailments. Some pills offer relief from depression, anxiety, or nervousness. Other medicines help people sleep, keep them awake, or give them energy. Millions of dollars are spent each year on drug advertising. Most ads promise instant relief—a quick fix. While many medicines are recommended by doctors, and promote good health, others are probably unnecessary. Some are even harmful if taken too much. When taking medications is part of daily life for so many adults, what message is sent to young people? The message is that taking pills and medicines will make you feel better, regardless of the problem. This kind of attitude sets the stage for illegal drug abuse—with the potential for disastrous results.

41

The New Woodstock Generation

Many LSD users in the Sixties took the drug to have a "spiritual experience." LSD today is often referred to as a party drug, because many users say it helps them relax and be more comfortable at parties and other social events. However, there is always a risk when a person takes LSD.

"While the adolescents we interviewed spent a great deal of time talking about good trips, they also talked about bad ones," said researcher Michael Agar, Ph.D. "Sometimes users had bad trips that reached nightmarish proportions. The profoundly bad trips that were described all had an element in common: They all involved loss of control. Profoundly bad trips can cause a user to quit. The fear of having another bad experience can overwhelm their desire to use the drug again."[11]

Concerts, Raves, and LSD

The connection between LSD and rock music remains strong. LSD is popular at rock concerts, where sound and light shows seem even more spectacular through an acid haze. DEA agents believe that rock concerts often serve as distribution centers for LSD. As a result, concerts have been the scene of many LSD arrests over the past few years.

LSD and other drugs are also abused at raves, all-night dance parties attended by large groups of young adults. Many raves are held in warehouses, lofts, or other large spaces.

Raves began in Europe in the late 1980s, and have recently spread to the United States. At first, raves were held in secret. They were illegal, so nobody advertised them. People found out about raves through roadside signs and word of mouth. Now,

42

raves are held openly and legally in clubs and stadiums. Some raves attract hundreds, even thousands of people.[12]

At raves, loud, fast music plays nonstop. Electronic "bridge" music fills the spaces between songs, so people can dance without interruption. The loud music, flashing lights, and huge crowds of dancers gives the rave scene a feeling of raw energy.

The average age of rave-goers is eighteen.[13] However, some are as young as fourteen or fifteen, and some are in their twenties or thirties. LSD, marijuana, and other drugs are sold openly at raves. The cheaper drugs, such as LSD, are among the most popular. In a survey of people at a rave, three-quarters said they

Raves, or all-night dance parties, are popular in many parts of the United States, Canada, and Europe. Roadside signs like these tell teenagers when and where raves will be. Drugs, particularly LSD and marijuana, are a significant part of the rave scene.

were using one or more drugs.[14] Drugs are just as much a part of the rave scene as music and dancing. Most people probably would not have the energy to dance nonstop all night if they were not high on some kind of drug.

Changes in Family Life

While the number of teens who attend raves is relatively small, the fact is that today's young people have much more freedom than their parents did. Family life has changed a great deal in the last thirty-five years. Perhaps the biggest change is the increase of women in the workplace. The "apple pie" family where the father works and the mother stays home is becoming a thing of the past. Today, 68 percent of mothers with children under eighteen work outside the home. Many children are on their own for hours after school. They become used to having freedom and making their own decisions.[15] However, the decisions they make may not always be the best ones for them.

Parents, even those who may not have much time to spend with their kids, must learn to set limits. Setting limits means saying no when a teen wants to do something a parent does not approve of. Teens are in the process of separating from their parents and learning how to be adults.[16] They usually want a lot of freedom as they start to separate from their parents. Conflicts often arise as parents try to decide how much freedom to allow teens.

Many parents have trouble setting limits. Sometimes they are not sure when to say no. Other times they give in to their teens' demands because they are tired of constant fights over staying out late or using the car. While too little freedom can harm normal development, too much freedom may put a teen in dangerous situations.

Consequences of LSD Use

The teen years are a time for taking risks and trying new things. While teens may feel that nothing will happen to them, this is not always the case, especially with a drug as unpredictable as LSD. Driving a car or even walking across the street is dangerous while tripping on acid. Not knowing the facts about LSD can have many negative results.

"Even if we could put a warning label on LSD, telling people not to swim, operate a boat, or drive a car while taking the drug, it wouldn't help," said Richard H. Schwartz, M.D., a pediatrician who has studied adolescent LSD use. "Kids on LSD aren't concerned with following the rules, and they won't be reading labels very carefully."[17]

Most young people who abuse drugs have one thing in common: They experiment with many different drugs. Compulsive drug abusers—people who have an almost uncontrollable need to take drugs—often choose to take LSD. While many say LSD is their favored drug, it is not the only one they use. LSD abusers also report high levels of marijuana and alcohol use.

Another danger of LSD abuse is its possible link with teenage suicide, a leading cause of death in teens. New statistics show large increases of suicide among children ages ten to fourteen. Drug abuse is considered one of the major stresses leading to teen suicide.[18] LSD use may cause severe depression. Teens who are already depressed risk feeling like committing suicide after taking LSD.

Today, most health professionals are strongly against experimenting with LSD for any reason. There are too many reasons why it is an unsafe substance. Buying LSD from unknown people is particularly risky. In a recent study of drug users, 21 percent of those studied took LSD three days in a row, and 40 percent took three doses or more simultaneously.[19] "We're starting to see another upswing in drug use," said David Smith, M.D., founder of a San Francisco drug treatment clinic. "And another whole new generation is experimenting with hallucinogens. They are using themselves as experimental laboratories for strange drug combinations that no scientist ever thought of."[20] Whether it is taken with other drugs or alone, LSD is unpredictable and dangerous—and the results of abuse are disastrous.

Laws Against LSD

There are both state and federal laws against LSD. Every state has laws prohibiting use, possession, and sale of the drug. In addition, the federal government has outlawed LSD by listing it under Schedule 1 of the Controlled Substances Act. Schedule 1 includes all drugs that have no accepted medical use and are likely to be abused.[21]

The Controlled Substances Act provides penalties for those who manufacture and distribute drugs. The more dangerous the drug and the larger the quantity involved, the stiffer the penalty. Anyone found trafficking, or dealing LSD can be fined millions of dollars, depending on how much of the drug is involved.[22]

Possession of one to ten grams of LSD with intent to distribute can send a person to prison for at least five years. Possession of ten or more grams would send a person to prison for ten years. Because LSD is a mixture, the weight of what it is mixed with, and the substance it is stored on, is included when

There are strict laws against use, possession, and sale of LSD. Violating these laws can lead to stiff penalties. For example, someone possessing just a small amount of LSD can be sent to jail for five years or more.

calculating a prison term. So people arrested on LSD charges may get longer prison terms than those caught with other drugs.

One person serving time in prison for LSD charges, Logan Martin, was arrested at an Ohio rock concert two years ago while carrying fifty doses of LSD in his wallet. Martin is currently serving a four- to fifteen-year prison term even though he had never been arrested for a crime before. His claim that he did not plan to sell the LSD did not reduce his sentence.[23]

John McKean, another Ohio resident, is serving a seven- to twenty-five year sentence for selling a hundred doses of LSD to a coworker. The wood factory employee bought the LSD at a rock concert at the coworker's request. "Someone at work had been bugging me to bring acid back, and I was stupid and I did it. I'm not saying what I did was right, but I hadn't been dealing at all," he said. "I just did it as a favor." The coworker, who was also arrested, received a reduced sentence because she gave evidence against McKean.[24]

According to the Bureau of Statistics, average federal sentences for LSD offenses are higher than sentences for many violent crimes. Because the penalties for LSD are so severe, being caught using or selling the drug can ruin your life.

Questions for Discussion

1. Why do you think society is so dependent on pills? What alternate methods are there for people to overcome pain?

2. There seems to be a strong correlation between rock music and drugs. Why do think this is so? Do you know anyone who feels they have to be high in order to have a good time at a concert or rave?

3. Penalties for LSD possesion are severe. Why do you think they are so stiff? Do you think it is fair that the punishment for LSD possesion is more severe than for some other types of crimes?

4

The Faces Behind LSD Abuse

It is hard to describe today's typical LSD user, because there really is no such thing as a typical user. Many different kinds of people take LSD. "It isn't just the offbeat kids with their hair dyed purple who are using LSD," said Joan Goodman, a social worker who counsels LSD users. "It's also what I call the 'apple pie' kids—the clean-cut ones who do well in school and seem to have no problems at all. They're bright, get good grades, and are often very popular. At the same time, they feel under pressure, so they turn to LSD and other drugs to relieve some of the stress."[1]

There are a few things you should know about abusers of LSD, and other drugs. Many are in their late teens or early twenties. They are usually white males from the suburbs.[2] Many are from middle-class or upper-middle-class families.

Drug Use: Ages and Stages

Alcohol, tobacco, and marijuana are often referred to as gateway drugs, because they frequently lead to stronger substances. Patterns of drug use can begin as early as the elementary school years, and continue on through college.

Elementary School. Use of LSD and other drugs is uncommon in grade school. Many students may try alcohol and tobacco. While these are legal substances for adults, they are illegal and dangerous for young children. Thirty percent of children drink alcohol for the first time between the ages of nine and twelve, and nearly 10 percent have tried alcohol by the sixth grade.[3]

Younger students often say they have a beer or smoke a cigarette out of curiosity. Since children of this age are very influenced by parents and teachers, elementary school is the time to begin prevention programs, with particular emphasis on alcohol and tobacco.[4]

Middle School. Patterns of drug abuse increase greatly during the middle- or junior-high-school years. In one study, 67 percent of eighth graders reported using alcohol and 45 percent had smoked cigarettes. While alcohol and tobacco continue to be popular, many students report experimenting with marijuana, inhalants, and amphetamines as well. Only 3 percent had tried LSD.[5]

Many students do not see the harm in using alcohol, tobacco, and marijuana. They mistakenly think it is a sign of growing up. This age group is heavily influenced by what their friends think, say, and do. Following the group is more important to them than listening to parents or teachers.

High School. By tenth grade, almost 81 percent reported using alcohol, 56 percent had smoked cigarettes, and 6 percent had used LSD. Drug abuse continued to increase through the high school years, but the rate of increase began to slow down. By the twelfth grade, 87 percent reported drinking alcohol, 62 percent smoked cigarettes, and 10 percent used LSD.[6]

College. Drug abuse is widespread at many colleges. Ninety-four percent of college students reported using alcohol and 66 percent have smoked cigarettes. LSD use among college students remained steady at 10 percent.[7]

College students are regarded as adults, even though many are still teenagers living away from home for the first time. Many college students are too young to legally drink alcohol. Because so many college students abuse drugs, drug education should continue through the college years.

Facts and Figures on LSD Use

"Young people living in suburban areas are the primary users of LSD and hallucinogens," said Special Agent Ronald Brogan of the DEA. "While LSD is the most commonly used hallucinogen, people who take LSD tend to use other hallucinogenic drugs as well."[8] LSD is especially popular in the northwestern states—California, Washington, and Oregon—probably because most of the world's supply of LSD and other hallucinogens is manufactured in that area.[9]

More males than females tend to experiment with LSD and hallucinogens. In fact, males are more likely to use any illegal drugs, and to be heavy drug users.[10] One study found that 11.8 percent of the male population had used hallucinogens, as compared to 5.9 percent of the female population.[11]

Whites use LSD and hallucinogens more than any other ethnic group. The number of black and Hispanic people who use hallucinogens is much lower. One survey found that 10.1 percent of whites had tried hallucinogens, as compared to 5.9 percent of Hispanics and only 3 percent of blacks.[12]

Education is another factor in the abuse of LSD and other drugs. In general, the more educated a person is, the less likely he or she is to take drugs. People who are college graduates use drugs less than people who do not graduate from college. Most illegal drug use peaks before the senior year of high school.

However, LSD and other hallucinogens are exceptions to this rule. Many young people, especially males, continue to use hallucinogenic drugs through their twenties and even into their thirties. One survey found that hallucinogens were used by 15.2 percent of eighteen- to twenty-five-year-old males, and by 19.7 percent of twenty-six- to thirty-four-year-old males.[13]

First Steps Towards Drugs

"The first time I ever got high, it was on beer. I was twelve years old," said Stephanie Cooper*, a seventeen-year-old from New Jersey. "I never liked alcohol much, but I liked being high. So I started drinking regularly, every day. We'd drink at school, and I'd sneak out at night to get drunk. After awhile, drinking got boring, so I started smoking weed [marijuana]."[14]

The progression from alcohol to marijuana is typical for many young people. Thirty-five percent of all high-school seniors have used marijuana sometime during high school.[15] Like many other drug users, Stephanie did not stop with marijuana.

*Not her real name.

"I smoked weed for awhile, then tried a lot of different drugs, including LSD, mescaline [another hallucinogen], angel dust, and cocaine," she said. "Once I started using drugs regularly, they became an important part of my life."[16]

Why Teens Get High

There is no single reason why young people abuse drugs. A Minneapolis-based drug counselor recently asked a group of teens to raise their hands if they used drugs because of peer pressure, family or school problems, or just because it was fun. Most of the teenagers raised their hands for all three reasons.[17]

Some people use drugs to fit in. They want to be liked and accepted by others. If a friend offers them drugs, they might say "yes" because they want to fit in with a certain crowd. They fail to realize that no drug can change who they are.

Some people think drugs will help them escape from an unhappy home life, problems getting along with parents or friends, and poor performance in school. LSD changes how someone sees reality, so it might look appealing to people who want their lives to be different. In reality, the problems that LSD creates are far worse than the original problems a user was trying to escape.

For teenagers who are bored, LSD may appear to be an exciting and stimulating experience. There are, however, many other ways for teens to have fun and safely express themselves.

Shy people may think that drugs help them loosen up. They may lose some of their inhibitions and feel more relaxed. However, teens who think LSD is a social drug soon find that they are wrong. "LSD helps the user appreciate objects and images, but not groups of people. When you are tripping, you're

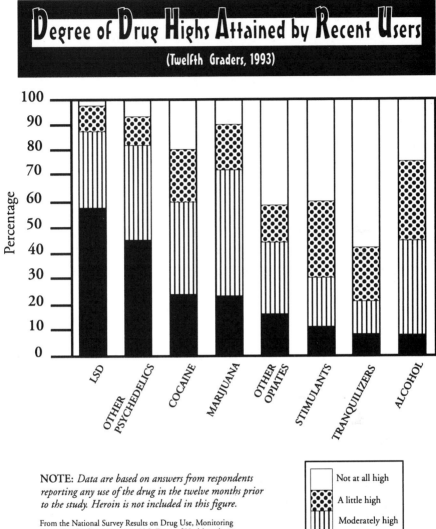

Degree of Drug Highs Attained by Recent Users

(Twelfth Graders, 1993)

Percentage

LSD — OTHER PSYCHEDELICS — COCAINE — MARIJUANA — OTHER OPIATES — STIMULANTS — TRANQUILIZERS — ALCOHOL

NOTE: *Data are based on answers from respondents reporting any use of the drug in the twelve months prior to the study. Heroin is not included in this figure.*

From the National Survey Results on Drug Use, Monitoring the Future Study, 1975–1993; U.S. Dept. of Health and Human Services.

Not at all high
A little high
Moderately high
Very high

Although there are many factors that influence teen drug use, LSD is particularly popular because, out of the drugs teens tend to experiment with, its high is among the most intense.

in your own little world. It's not going to help you connect with your friends in any real way," said a pediatrician who has studied LSD users.[18]

Stephanie expressed the feeling that it was okay to do drugs because her parents did them. "My dad used to drink a lot. He also smokes a lot of weed," said Stephanie. "As soon as he comes home from work, he gets high. So when my parents would tell me to stop using drugs, I'd say, 'Dad gets high—why shouldn't I?'"[19] While parents should act as role models for their kids, this unfortunately is not always the case. However, having a poor role model is not a reason for teens to abuse drugs.

Tripping With Friends

Even though LSD is not a social drug, people usually take it in groups rather than alone. "The influence of friends is a major reason why teenagers try LSD—or any other drug—for the first time," said Bill Alden, deputy director of D.A.R.E., a nationwide drug education program for middle- and high-school students.[20]

Stephanie's first LSD experience was with her friends. "I was fourteen when I tried LSD for the first time," she recalled:

> One of my friends gave me some blotter. Whenever I took LSD, it was with this same group of friends. I didn't get along with my parents, so my friends were like my family. I spent a lot of time with them, hanging around and doing drugs. By the time I was fourteen years old, drugs and partying were my entire life. I never had any money to buy drugs, but that wasn't a problem. My friends gave them to me. The people I hung around with were older than I was.

We partied all the time, at clubs, people's apartments, even hotel rooms. Hotel parties were fun. We'd rent a big room, get high on acid or other drugs, listen to music, and play cards. Nobody would sleep—the drugs kept us up. But the next day, I'd be exhausted, especially if I did LSD. I'd come home and stay in bed the entire day. My parents would be furious, but there was nothing they could do.[21]

No Parental Authority

Teens might think of turning to drugs and alcohol if their parents do not get along, fight a lot, separate, or get divorced. Getting high may seem like a way of escaping family problems—it is not.

"I started using drugs right after my parents split up," remembered Stephanie. "I lived with my Mom at the time, but we were constantly fighting. I would sneak out of the house every night to get high. No matter how carefully she locked the doors and windows, I'd still find a way to get out. We fought so much that she finally kicked me out. That's when I went to live with my Dad."[22]

Problems often arise when parents cannot agree on how to raise their children. If parents have different rules, teens are not sure whose rules to follow. Often, they end up doing what they want.[23] Stephanie said, "My Mom was really strict. But my Dad had no rules at all. I preferred living with him, so I could do what I wanted."[24]

In a recent study, many students said their parents knew they used alcohol, tobacco, and marijuana, but did not try to stop them. The parents believed that eventually their children would

HE'S THE IMAGE OF HIS FATHER.

People who turn kids onto drugs aren't always the dregs of the earth. They're people who love children more than anything. Parents.

Everything mothers and fathers do, no matter how discreet, leaves a lasting impression on sons and daughters. With millions of parents doing drugs, it's no wonder millions of kids are doing the same.

So if you're wondering where children pick up their habits, where in the world they get them from, you don't have to look very far. It's you.

IF PARENTS STOP, KIDS WON'T START.

Partnership for a Drug-Free America.

Children of drug users are more likely to use drugs than children whose parents avoid drugs and alcohol. Posters like this one emphasize how important it is for parents to be healthy role models for their children.

give up drugs on their own. Other students in the study said their parents allowed them to use these drugs, as long as they did not move on to the "harder" substances.[25]

When parents of teenage drug users do not set limits, the teen is in control, instead of the parents.[26] "Things got so bad that neither of my parents could tell me what to do," Stephanie said. "If they told me not to go out at night, I'd say 'Try and stop me.' Then I'd run away from home for a few days."[27]

Effects on Schoolwork

Schoolwork can be forgotten if LSD abuse becomes a habit. Students who abuse drugs have other things on their minds besides getting an education. Skipping school or cutting class can become common. Since LSD causes a lack of sleep, users are usually exhausted after tripping.

In a recent study of adolescent LSD users, a majority said that school and LSD are not a good combination. Tripping in school made them lose the control they needed to learn. One teen said, "I remember being in geometry class once, taking a test, and I couldn't remember any of it. The words and images on the paper were like scrambling, and there was stuff coming out of the paper . . ."[28]

Dropping out of school is another serious consequence of heavy drug use. While students drop out for a variety of reasons, drug use is high on the list. Studies show that high-school dropouts use more drugs than students who stay in school.[29] They are also more likely to commit serious crimes. When students who abuse drugs leave school, they lose the opportunity to get an education. They also are unable to benefit from school-based drug prevention programs, even though they have the most to gain from them.

LSD Lifestyle

Many people who use LSD believe that they can control the drug. However, the drug usually ends up controlling them. For many LSD users, the drug takes over their lives. A typical trip lasts up to ten hours. It is an intense and exhausting experience. Afterward, the user needs several hours of sleep. There is little time or energy left for school or family matters.

"By the time I was fifteen, my entire life revolved around drugs," Stephanie remembered. "I got high every single day, sometimes on LSD, sometimes on other drugs. My habit was expensive. To make money, I started selling LSD. I'd take the bus to New York City, buy sheets of blotter, and bring it back to New Jersey. Nobody in my town sold acid, and there was a lot of demand for the drug. I had steady business, selling mostly to people I knew, or to friends of friends."[30]

Even though selling LSD is against the law, many young people do not take antidrug laws seriously. "They see drug dealers, primarily other students, openly disobeying the law and getting away with it. They have little respect for the police or others in a position of authority who do little to stop obviously illegal activities of fellow students."[31] At some point, however, drug abuse will have serious consequences.

Says Stephanie, "Eventually . . . I was arrested for possession of marijuana. I'm still facing these charges, and I may end up going to jail."[32]

Spreading Bad News

How would you feel if someone gave you LSD without telling you, and you got high as a result? It may seem strange to think that a person would do something like that. However, it does happen. People have been known to "slip" others LSD without informing them.

"There has been an increase in the popularity of 'blunts,' or large, cigar-shaped marijuana joints," said Robert Johnson, M.D. "Sometimes, these 'blunts' contain LSD. When someone smokes the joint, they feel the effects of the LSD as well as the marijuana. The resulting high can be very intense."[33]

"We have heard about instances of LSD users 'flaking' others," said Assistant Special Agent Thomas Sheehan. "This term refers to giving someone drugs without telling them. In one case, someone carried liquid LSD in a plastic eyedrop bottle, and put a few drops of the drug into people's drinks when they weren't looking. It's a terrible thing to do to someone. But users see it as just another way to spread the drug around."[34]

Other Effects of LSD

There is no proof that taking LSD leads anyone to commit crimes. However, heavy use of LSD and other drugs is the cause of many problems for families and society. Drug-related crimes are responsible for much of the violence in American neighborhoods and schools. Use of drugs often results in personal tragedy as well.

Teens who use LSD and other drugs often do not realize they have a problem. They do not see their drug use as negative behavior. Their parents and teachers are usually the first to realize there is a problem. Often, an LSD user's grades decline. Attendance at school drops, too. The teenager could even be caught stealing.

"I've broken into stores to steal money for drugs," said Stephanie. "Once I even stole money from my grandmother. At the time, I didn't see anything wrong with what I did. Now, though, I realize it was wrong."[35]

A change in behavior may also indicate an LSD problem. One parent knew something was wrong when her fifteen-year-old son gave up hockey, a sport he had played—and loved—since he was ten. When she asked him why he dropped the sport, he said, "I just don't like it anymore." The next day, she took him to a counselor. She did not know he was taking LSD or any other drug. But the fact that he had given up his favorite activity was cause for concern. The problem was, in fact, LSD and other drugs.[36]

Drugs, including LSD, are responsible for other behavior problems, both at school and at home. Many teenage abusers have angry relationships with people in authority, such as parents and teachers. Poor grades, school suspensions, and arrests are common. In a Virginia survey of teenage LSD abusers at a drug treatment facility, 92 percent had been brought in by their parents for out-of-control behavior, including fighting, skipping school, and failing in school.[37]

Shattered Families, Wasted Lives

Stephanie's experiences with LSD were mostly negative. "My first trip was great, but all the others were bad," she said. "I almost killed myself trying to recapture that first good feeling, but it never came back. Most times, LSD made me feel really down and depressed. That's why I finally gave it up."[38]

Stephanie has not experienced flashbacks since she stopped using LSD. She has been lucky. Many acid abusers suffer from panic attacks, hallucinations, nightmares, and other problems. In one study, 64 percent of teenage LSD users said they saw flashbacks after taking the drug. Many of the flashbacks, mostly light trails, geometric shapes, and halos around objects, were not frightening. However, 16 percent reported seeing frightening flashbacks. For two abusers, frightening flashbacks occurred daily for a year or more.[39]

"Taking LSD is like playing Russian roulette," says Bonnie C. Kauder, director of adolescent ambulatory programs at Phoenix House Foundation. "You never know when you'll have a really bad trip that may affect you for the rest of your life. I knew someone who took only one LSD trip. Unfortunately, it was a bad one. He never recovered from it."[40]

"If someone asked me if taking LSD and other drugs was worth it, I'd have to say definitely not," said Stephanie. "It's really messed me up. My whole family has suffered as a result of my drug use. My two younger brothers don't want to have anything to do with me. I've missed out on being a normal teenager, on owning my first car, and going to the prom. I'll never have the chance to do these things.

"What does the future hold for me? I'm a high school dropout, facing a jail term. I'm glad I'm in rehab, but part of me still wants to do drugs. I'm almost eighteen years old—I have to get my life together before it's too late."[41]

Questions for Discussion

1. What preventative measures do you think parents and schools should take to warn children about the dangers of LSD?

2. LSD has been slipped to some people without their knowledge. What can you do to ensure that something like that does not happen to you?

3. What are some ways teens who have problems at home can cope so that they do not turn to LSD or other drugs?

5

LSD and Families

Each year, more than one million American families are affected by a drug problem. Some families confront the problem and try to solve it. Others suffer in silence—either because they do not know what to do or because they are too embarrassed to look for help. Some family members may even help hide or make up for the user's actions in any number of ways. They are responsible for making it possible for drug abuse to continue. These people are called codependents. Often, they do not even realize that they are supporting the user's habit.

Teens who abuse LSD cause their families great pain and anxiety. Any involvement with drugs is worrisome, but LSD use is of particular concern. Its effects are often quite severe. LSD users have lost control of their lives. Most are polydrug users (they use many drugs). They take different drugs together without worrying much about the consequences. Getting high is the focal point of their lives. Many drug counselors refer to them as the most alienated of all drug users.

Coping with an adolescent LSD abuser is often so stressful for families that many avoid the problem or pretend it does not exist. Society holds parents responsible for the behavior of their children. Therefore, many parents blame themselves when a child becomes involved with drugs. They are ashamed and embarrassed, believing that they have failed as parents. They feel that somehow their child's drug abuse must be their fault.

There are no studies proving that LSD use is inherited from a parent. Many experts believe that both genetics and environment, or home life, are factors in abuse of alcohol and drugs in general. Research shows that if parents abuse alcohol or drugs (either illegal or prescription), their children are likely to do so, too. Children of regular alcohol users are also more likely to use drugs than children whose parents do not drink much.

The influence of mothers may be particularly strong regarding drug abuse. In one study of mothers who were cigarette smokers and/or moderate drinkers, their teenage children were more likely to use a variety of drugs.[1]

Since many behaviors are learned from our parents, the example set at home is a very important one. Parents who avoid illegal drugs, do not smoke and drink, or drink only small amounts, are healthy role models for their children.

Discovering the Problem

"LSD users—and *all* drug users—are con artists," said one drug counselor. "They try to protect their habit any way they can.

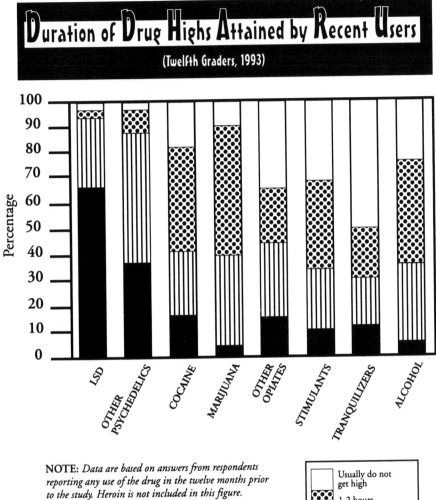

Duration of Drug Highs Attained by Recent Users
(Twelfth Graders, 1993)

NOTE: *Data are based on answers from respondents reporting any use of the drug in the twelve months prior to the study. Heroin is not included in this figure.*

From the National Survey Results on Drug Use, Monitoring the Future Study, 1975–1993; U.S. Dept. of Health and Human Services.

Legend:
- Usually do not get high
- 1-2 hours
- 3-6 hours
- 7 or more hours

Studies have shown that LSD is a popular drug among high schoolers because it is the drug they feel gives them the longest-lasting high. This long-lasting high allows more time for escape from issues young people are having difficulty dealing with.

However, observant parents can pick up signals. The thing to look for is any major change in behavior. A teenager who has always been talkative and outgoing suddenly becomes withdrawn. A good eater picks at food or avoids meals altogether. A student athlete quits the team for no apparent reason."[2]

Jill, a teenage LSD user, was rebellious and defiant. She dyed her hair, wore white pancake makeup, and dressed in black, including combat boots. Jill went out with her friends every night, but lied to her parents about where she was going. When they found out, they became angry and told her she had to stay home. Jill began sneaking out after they were asleep. Eventually she was caught. During their many fights about her behavior, Jill would always tell her parents she hated them.

One morning, after tripping all night at a friend's house, Jill called her father just to tell him she loved him. Jill's phone call indicated a dramatic change in her behavior. Unfortunately, her father did not recognize Jill's words as a "red flag." Her parents never caught on to the warning signs she gave them that indicated she used LSD. After repeated suspensions from school, Jill was finally placed on a home detention monitoring program. She later underwent counseling for her drug problem.[3]

The following types of behavior may also suggest that a teenager may be using LSD:
- *dropping old friends for a new crowd*
- *any change in eating habits; weight gain or loss*
- *mood swings, depression, or irritability*
- *declining grades and poor attendance at school*
- *paranoid behavior and panic attacks*
- *extreme tiredness or disruption of sleep patterns*
- *secretive behavior or insistence on privacy*

Families Under Stress

It may be easy to hide the physical evidence of LSD use from parents. However, behavior changes are not so easily hidden. Rebellious, out-of-control behavior is an important symptom of acid use. An LSD user's mood swings, anger, and defiance affect the entire family.

If someone you know—a friend or family member—is on acid, you may have found that it can be stressful to deal with them. They may be difficult to talk to because they often do not want to listen to anybody: parents, peers, or teachers. They may sneak out at night, stay out all night, or come home high. They may steal money, or take household items to sell or trade for drugs. Sometimes they get arrested or have auto accidents while tripping. Family fights may be frequent occurrences.

Siblings can be particularly affected by a brother's or sister's LSD use. Parents are often so preoccupied by the drug problem that they may pay less attention to other family matters. Siblings who have to live with frequent fights and tension may turn to drugs, too, in an effort to gain their parents' attention. Others, like the younger brothers of Stephanie Cooper (see Chapter 4), may avoid drugs completely. They may be totally turned off, having already seen firsthand how drugs destroy lives and families, how everyone becomes a victim of the LSD user's behavior.

"Not My Child"

It is often very difficult for parents to accept the fact that a child may be using LSD or any other drug. They may not want to face such an unpleasant reality, even when the signs are obvious. So, some parents look for other ways to explain a teen's behavior problems. Many blame the behavior on the mood swings of adolescence. However, there is a difference between normal adolescent rebellion and behavior that is out of control. Most teens have disagreements and conflicts with their parents. However, only a small minority stay out all night, come home high, wreck cars, or steal money.

Parents who do not talk to their teenagers about these behavior changes are sending the message that the behavior is acceptable. "The signs of drug use are always there. When parents ignore these signs and don't take action, it's a non-verbal sign of approval," said one counselor.[4]

Sometimes parents suspect that a child is using LSD, but are not absolutely sure. They may hold back because they do not want to jump to conclusions or accuse anyone unfairly. Drug counselors say that parents should talk about *any* major behavior changes with their children. If the problem is not drugs, it may be something else. Whatever is wrong needs to be addressed.

Facing the Facts

A drug abuser's apparent out-of-control behavior is often an attempt to let people know that help is needed. Unfortunately, by the time a parent discovers a problem with LSD, it is likely to be serious. The odds are strong that the teen has been using LSD and many other drugs for quite some time. The drug habit is probably well established.

Parents may feel hurt and guilty when they learn that their teenager is using LSD. They may also be frightened. Perhaps they have heard frightening stories about LSD. Parents usually know the risks of taking acid but often may be reluctant to confront a child. They hope the drug use is only a stage and they want to avoid an unpleasant confrontation.

By not speaking up about LSD use, parents allow the drug abuser to remain in control. Family life revolves around the abuser's behavior, and everyone feels angry and resentful because of it. "Parents need to remember that they have power," says a counselor. "Being the parents gives them power. But they can't be afraid to use it."[5]

Intervention

If you or someone you know is involved with LSD, there are places to find help. The first step toward solving the problem is admitting that it exists. You can talk to your parents or to another adult you trust. Using LSD is dangerous. Drug use of any kind is unacceptable, and so is the behavior that accompanies it. Drug use affects the whole family, not just the user.

If you use LSD, you may find it difficult to admit there is a problem. You may not want to talk about it. It is easier, when friends or family members intervene, to deny everything or say the situation is under control. Even when you are high, you may think you can compose yourself enough to act "straight" around parents and teachers.[6]

At first, parents may not want to face the facts, so they may accept denials. However, eventually the truth sinks in. If the LSD user continues to deny drug abuse, family conflicts may become worse.[7]

Interventions between LSD users and parents are likely to be angry. Users do not want to be found out. They want to continue taking drugs. They know their parents want to avoid

71

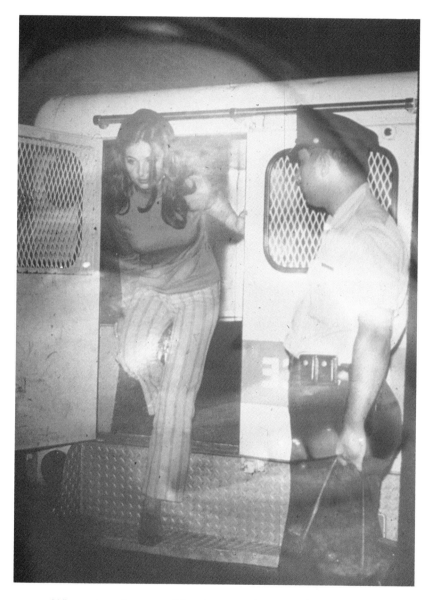

When a teen is arrested for drug use, the entire family suffers. Many teenage drug offenders are sent to drug treatment facilities by the courts as part of their sentence.

unpleasantness, so they shout and become abusive in an effort to end the discussion.

"It's important for parents to hold their ground and not back down," said a drug counselor. "Don't accept any excuses from the child, and don't make any compromises. Take control of the situation, and don't be intimidated by shouts and anger."[8]

Parents need to emphasize that they love the child, but not the behavior. In order for the family to function, the LSD use and problem behavior must stop. A calm, straightforward approach works best. Counselors advise parents to follow these steps:

- *Do not become angry or emotional. Do not raise your voice.*
- *Do not put a drug user on the defensive.*
- *Avoid confronting a child who comes home at 1 or 2 A.M., high on drugs. Save the discussion for the next day.*

Families of LSD users need to change their own attitudes and behavior. They may have looked the other way for a long time, allowing the LSD user to disrupt family life. With intervention, they can begin to regain control of their lives.

Learning and talking about drug abuse allows family members to address their problems in a healthy and productive way. No matter how serious the crisis, help is available.

Finding Help

LSD users and their families looking for help may not be sure where to find it. Many families find help from the sources on the following pages.

Doctors: In a drug crisis, many parents will first call their pediatrician or family doctor. A doctor can be helpful, particularly if he or she has known the teen for a long time and they are comfortable with each other. Many physicians have limited experience in treating drug problems. However, even if they do not know much about LSD, they may be able to help families locate appropriate drug treatment and counseling programs.

Local Hospitals or Medical Centers: Many large health centers, particularly those in or near cities, offer drug treatment services to the public.

Substance Abuse Agencies: Government agencies will have information on drug and alcohol abuse, and can also supply the names of local treatment resources.

Counselors, Social Workers, and Therapists: Many professionals are trained to treat drug abusers and their families with individual, family, and group therapy.

Teachers, Principals, or Guidance Counselors: School officials are usually experienced in dealing with teen drug abuse, and can provide referrals for treatment and counseling.

Hotlines: Some communities and drug treatment centers offer twenty-four-hour hotlines that family members can call for information. Trained operators take phone calls and make referrals, but they are not qualified to offer medical information or advice.

Peer-Group Assistance

When faced with a drug problem, whether it is LSD or any other substance, many people turn to their peers for help. They talk to friends and neighbors, especially those who also have had a family member with a drug problem. Or they find peer support through self-help organizations. Families gain strength in seeing how others, both friends and strangers, cope with drug abuse.

Self-help organizations sponsor meetings where families

can give each other advice and emotional support. While there are no self-help groups specifically for families of LSD users, there are many for families of drug users. Three such groups are Families Anonymous (based in Culver City, California), Nar-Anon World (based in Palos Verdes Peninsula, California), and Parent to Parent (based in Marietta, Georgia).

Families Anonymous (FA) is based on the twelve-step program originally developed by Alcoholics Anonymous in 1935. Over the years, Alcoholics Anonymous (AA) has helped millions of alcoholics stop drinking. By following a series of twelve steps, alcoholics learn to face their problem and stay sober. The twelve-step program works so well that other organizations, including FA, have adapted it to help others.

In FA, the twelve steps are for the family members of drug abusers, not the drug abusers themselves. Years ago, "families" usually referred to parents of teenage drug users. Today, FA is multigenerational (including many generations of family members) in its approach. Many members are grandparents of abusers, or parents of adult drug abusers.

FA meetings are open to anyone who has a family member with a drug problem. At the meetings, people talk about their experiences, listen to others, and learn new ways of coping with the problem behavior of drug abusers. The focus of the program is on the family, not the user. Family members learn to rebuild their lives and find peace, whether or not the drug abuser stops taking drugs.

The slogan for AA is:
- *Who you see here*
- *What you see here*
- *When you leave here*
- *Let it stay here.*[9]

Like AA, FA also guarantees confidentiality. No last names are used. Members feel safe in talking about their experiences. They do not have to worry that others will gossip about them or repeat their stories.

FA has more than five hundred groups in fifteen countries. Anyone interested in attending their meetings can call or write the organization for information. They will be referred to a group in their area. Groups are organized by nonprofessionals, and there are no dues or membership fees.

Nar-Anon World is another organization giving emotional support to families of drug users. Members attend meetings and discuss ways to cope when a family member uses drugs. They learn that someone else's drug abuse is not their fault, and that they cannot prevent someone from abusing drugs.

Parent to Parent, a product of PRIDE (Parents' Resource Institute for Drug Education) teaches families strategies for dealing with teenage drug abuse. When a teenager uses drugs, many parents do not take action because they hold one or more of the following beliefs:

1. *"It's no big deal."*

2. *"There is nothing I can do."*

3. *"It won't happen to me."*

4. *"They are going to do it anyway."*

5. *"Everybody's doing it."*

6. *"They won't listen to me."*

7. *"I don't have time."*

8. *"The school will take care of it."*[10]

Parent to Parent calls these the eight fatal beliefs. Parents who believe these statements are not facing the facts about their child's drug abuse. Through a series of workshops, Parent to Parent helps parents understand why their children got involved with drugs and how drugs affect behavior. It also teaches them how to change their attitudes and take the necessary action to stop drug abuse.

Questions for Discussion

1. What are some signs that would indicate to parents that their child is using LSD?

2. Why do you think many parents look the other way even though they suspect their child is using LSD, or other drugs?

3. How do you think families should go about choosing a treatment program for an abuser in their household? State reasons why different treatments are effective for different families.

6

Treatment, Recovery, and Prevention

If you feel physically sick, you usually know where to turn for help. For a sore throat, you see the family doctor or pediatrician. For an earache, you make an appointment with an ear specialist. For a toothache, you see a dentist. For a sprain or possible broken bone, you go to an orthopedist.

Just as all illnesses are not the same and require different care, drug problems are also different from one another. People are different from one another, too. A drug treatment program that helps one person may not be right for another, even if they both abused the same drug. That is why it is necessary to check out all treatment options before making a decision.

Treating the Person, Not the Drug

Treatment for drug use is relatively new. Before the 1960s, few treatment programs existed. They were not believed to be effective or necessary. Back then, drug abuse was considered incurable. Instead of being treated, drug abusers and sellers were arrested and put in prison.

During the 1960s, when drug abuse became widespread among young people, treatment programs grew. Today, there are many different kinds of programs. The United States spends about $75 billion a year on health care for substance abuse. Some people recover, and some do not.

There are no drug treatment programs designed specifically for LSD users. Many programs treat the drug-taking behavior of a person, not the problems associated with specific drugs. Many drug abusers adopt a lifestyle that can best be described by the motto, "Live to use, use to live." Through counseling, users learn to change their attitudes and values. They also work on solving the emotional problems that led them to take drugs.

The Turning Point

Many young LSD users decide on their own to stop abusing drugs. They get tired of being high all the time, and do not want to be controlled by a drug. Some users are able to stop without outside help. Others need help from a counselor, therapist, or social worker. A well-established LSD habit will be very hard to break. In such a case, a drug rehabilitation program may offer the best treatment.

Some LSD users enter drug treatment programs involuntarily, because someone else has told them to. Sometimes parents insist on treatment. Other times, the courts insist on it. Users who are arrested for drug-related crimes often enter treatment programs as part of their sentence.

Sometimes users enter treatment programs after having a

medical emergency, usually a drug overdose. Overdosing on acid is rare. However, other LSD-related emergencies may require a visit to a hospital emergency room.

Bad trips. People having bad trips are anxious and panicky. They feel out of control and often worry that someone is out to harm them. Doctors who are experienced in treating negative LSD reactions use the "talk down" approach, talking quietly and reassuringly to calm the user.[1]

Talking down is very effective in calming the majority of people having bad trips. Once the effects of LSD wear off, they return to normal. They do not need medications.

A small number of users are too agitated to be talked down. They are treated with medications and physical restraint. (Physical restraint prevents disturbed patients from thrashing around, possibly harming themselves or others.) Doctors use medications such as sedatives or tranquilizers infrequently, because of negative side effects. Patients usually return to normal when the effects of the drug wear off. They seldom need to be hospitalized.

Acute intoxication. Occasionally LSD users take massive doses, or megadoses, of the drug, becoming very intoxicated, or high. This sometimes happens when powdered LSD is mistaken for cocaine and snorted, or sniffed through the nose.[2] Megadoses of LSD can result in loss of consciousness, seizures, and respiratory arrest. While this is rare, it is very dangerous.

Doctors will also try to talk down highly intoxicated patients. Medications and physical restraint are sometimes used if patients are agitated.

Prolonged adverse reactions. A typical LSD trip lasts for several hours. However, a small number of LSD users have bad trips that last much longer. These people often end up in the emergency room, where doctors will try to talk them down. If that does not work, they are given medications. In most instances, the effects of the drug eventually wear off. In a few cases, the bad trip lasts indefinitely, for weeks or even months. Extended medical help is then needed.[3]

There were two reported deaths from LSD in 1992. Both deaths resulted from dangerous behavior, not from toxic effects of the drug.[4]

Emergency room visits by LSD users have increased over the past decade. While most LSD users do not need to be hospitalized, any drug-related emergency that is severe enough to send the user to the emergency room is a cause for serious concern. When drug users come to the emergency room for medical treatment, doctors are not required to notify the police. However, most will recommend that the patient get treatment for drug abuse.

Types of Treatment

There are several treatment programs available for LSD abusers.

Short-term crisis intervention facilities are in hospitals. They usually treat people with serious drug reactions or overdoses. LSD users who are reacting to a combination of acid with other drugs may enter crisis intervention services. The length of stay varies from a few days to several weeks.

Inpatient programs are also in hospitals. LSD users with psychiatric problems are often admitted to hospitals for intensive counseling and psychiatric treatment. The length of stay varies from a few weeks to a few months.

Outpatient programs offer treatment for drug users without admission to a hospital. Many who choose outpatient treatment attend school or hold jobs. They go for counseling in the afternoons, evenings, and weekends, but still live at home. Some programs are very structured, with regular hours and scheduled sessions. Others have flexible hours. People come when they need help or advice. Family counseling is offered, usually once or twice a week. Patients stay in treatment for months and even years. Many programs offer long-term support from peers and counselors, through high school and even through college.

Residential treatment programs become a home away from home for many teenage drug abusers. The patient leaves home, family, friends, and school to live in a new drug-free environment. Many are placed in residential treatment programs after being arrested. Others are there because they have been unable to stop abusing drugs by any other method. Those with serious family problems often enter residential treatment centers when home life becomes too stressful.

Residential centers are supervised twenty-four hours a day. Patients attend school; go through individual, group, and family counseling; and sometimes work at the facility. Residential treatment programs are often considered a place of last resort for those with serious drug and behavior problems. The length of treatment ranges from a few months up to two years. After leaving a residential facility, patients often continue treatment at an outpatient facility.

Many counselors at drug treatment facilities are recovered drug abusers themselves. They receive special training to help others with drug problems.

Making the Right Choice

What type of treatment center is the best choice for a particular person? That depends on many factors, including:

83

- *the age and personality of the user*
- *how long the user has taken drugs*
- *how severe the drug problem is*
- *how motivated the user is to kick the habit*
- *the cost of treatment*

In general, the first attempt at drug treatment is usually the least restrictive and allows the most freedom. Using this guideline, users who have never undergone treatment may start with outpatient treatment first. Outpatient treatment allows an LSD user to remain at home and continue to attend school or work. It is often a good choice for teens who know they have a problem and want to get help. They will be motivated to attend counseling sessions and follow the program.

If someone on outpatient treatment continues to use LSD, a residential facility might be the next recommendation. Those with serious, well-established LSD habits may need more hands-on counseling than outpatient services provide. Gang members, or those who are dependent on drug-taking peers in other ways, are often placed in residential facilities, away from bad influences.

Sometimes, acid users with psychiatric problems are a danger to themselves or others. They are usually referred for inpatient treatment, possibly at a psychiatric hospital, and then go to a residential facility.

Residential facilities offer programs that include work or other job-skills training. Without learning specific skills, residents may become bored with the program. Job training gives a sense of responsibility. It also helps residents build new lives after drug treatment.

Research has shown that drug abusers from specific ethnic groups are more likely to recover if they are with peers from their ethnic group.[5] Since drug abuse affects all ethnic groups, treatment programs should be sensitive to cultural differences.

Pressure by parents to undergo treatment often results in resistance, even if the user really wants to change his or her behavior. Outpatient programs work best if there is a strong support system at home. When relations with parents are strained, or if both parents work long hours and are seldom home, a residential facility is probably a better choice.

Family counseling is considered an essential part of drug treatment. Family problems become worse when a family member abuses drugs. All family members need help in rebuilding relationships, strengthening communication, and building trust. If a family is unwilling or unable to participate in treatment, the user will often be referred to a residential treatment facility.

Treatment costs vary, depending on the type of treatment. Treatment at many public facilities is free. Private treatment can cost many thousands of dollars, depending on the length of stay. Most residential facilities cost thirty thousand dollars a year or more. Social service agencies and probation departments may pay some of the costs. Sometimes health insurance covers all or part of drug treatment. Many facilities will work with families so that treatment is affordable.

Recovery

All recovering LSD abusers need ongoing help and support, even if they have completed a drug treatment program. Recovering users can find the support they need from family, friends, and self-help organizations such as Narcotics Anonymous (NA).

NA, founded by a group of drug addicts in 1953, has helped thousands of people stop using drugs. In the Fifties, there were no self-help groups for drug users. As drug abuse became a more serious and widespread problem, many users began attending Alcoholics Anonymous meetings. A new organization, NA, was started to separate drug abusers from alcoholics. It offers help specifically for drug abusers.

NA is based on the twelve-step program of Alcoholics Anonymous. Anyone with a drug problem can join, and there are no dues or other costs. People learn to give up drugs by following a series of twelve steps. The goal is to give up drugs "for today." Giving up drugs "for today" is easier than giving them up for a lifetime.[6]

Most members have sponsors who come to meetings with them and provide emotional support. At meetings, drug abusers share their experiences. They learn new ways to avoid peer pressure and the temptation to abuse drugs again.

Every week, more than twenty thousand meetings are held across the United States and around the world. NA groups meet in twenty-four countries. The organization publishes printed materials in many languages.

Recovering drug abusers, both adults and teens, have to work hard at staying off drugs. Their lives are now drug-free, but not problem-free. Recovery brings many of the same stresses that led to drug abuse in the first place. Building self-esteem, making new, drug-free friends, finishing school, and deciding what to do next are all important.

Because of these pressures, relapses (getting high again) are common. A relapse does not necessarily mean that drug abuse will resume. However, repeated relapses may mean that more treatment is needed. It is not unusual to undergo treatment more than once. Changing behaviors and starting over takes time.

Prevention

"Treatment is the most difficult and expensive way to deal with the problems of drug abuse. Prevention is much cheaper and easier," said Gene R. Haislip of the Drug Enforcement Administration (DEA).[7]

Over the last two decades, a great effort has been made to reduce the abuse of illegal drugs in the United States. Prevention has been effective in reducing the problems of drug abuse. The use of all illegal substances by high school seniors has declined since the peak years of 1978–79. College students and young adults are "just saying no" in even greater numbers.

The war against drugs is being fought on many fronts. Parents, teachers, police, the medical community, the media, and the federal government are teaching Americans of all ages about the risks of drug abuse. Government, community groups, and law enforcement officials are working to remove drugs from America's neighborhoods and classrooms.

Parents need to talk to their children about the risks of drug abuse. "Schools, churches, synagogues, community groups, law enforcement—all can help us turn the tide on alcohol and drug abuse. But none can take a parent's place. Drug education must begin at home and in the neighborhood long before the classroom," said former President George Bush in 1991.[8]

It is also important for parents to set a healthy example by not abusing drugs or alcohol themselves. They should set firm limits about acceptable behavior. "I've heard many parents say, 'Know what you're swallowing,' or 'Taking drugs is okay as long as you tell me about it.' This is the wrong message. The right message is, 'Taking drugs is *never* okay,'" said one counselor.[9]

Schools and communities offer drug education programs for children of all ages, from kindergarten through high school. In many schools, drug education is part of the regular classroom curriculum, usually health or physical education classes.

One school-based program, Drug Abuse Resistance Education (D.A.R.E.), teaches students from kindergarten through high school about the risks of drug use. D.A.R.E., founded in 1983, is a program sponsored by schools and police departments. It reaches 5.5 million children in more than two hundred fifty thousand classrooms in the United States and many foreign countries. D.A.R.E. publishes educational materials for students, parents, and teachers. Large companies donate money to fund D.A.R.E. so schools do not have to pay for its programs.

D.A.R.E. trains local police officers to go into classrooms and teach courses in resisting drugs. The officers all have experience "on the streets," seeing firsthand the effects of drug and alcohol abuse. Most officers have also spent time working with children, often as volunteer coaches. The officers teach facts about drugs and alcohol, decision-making skills, and ways to resist peer pressure. The D.A.R.E. program is divided into four parts:

1. *Kindergarten Through Fourth Grade:* D.A.R.E. officers visit classrooms and meet students.

2. *Fifth/Sixth Grades:* D.A.R.E. officers teach students a seventeen-week curriculum about avoiding drugs and making positive, healthy choices.

3. *Junior High/Middle School:* Ten follow-up lessons, reinforcing what was learned in fifth and sixth grades.

4. *High School:* Nine new lessons that teach young people how to cope with real-life situations.

The core of the D.A.R.E. curriculum is taught in fifth and sixth grades, the time when many students feel peer pressure to try drugs and alcohol. D.A.R.E. officers spend time outside the classroom as well. They visit schools during lunch and recess and go on field trips and other special events.

Not everyone agrees with the D.A.R.E. approach. Some teachers believe that teaching is best left to teachers, and that police officers belong on the streets, not in classrooms. However, D.A.R.E.'s real-life approach appeals to many children. "Officer Myers is cool," said one sixth grader about his D.A.R.E. officer. "He doesn't just say, 'Drugs are bad. Don't do them.' Instead, he tells us what really happens to people who use drugs."[10]

Local police and law enforcement officials also work on their own to remove drugs from their communities. A group of police officers from Columbus, Ohio, formed a rock group called Hot Pursuit. They have performed at rock concerts for hundreds of thousands of teenagers across the country. All their music has an antidrug theme.[11]

Schools are involved in many programs that teach students to avoid drugs. Middle schools and high schools sponsor drug-free dances and sporting events for students. Other schools make drug- and alcohol-free proms a high priority. Communities across the United States support Project Graduation, sponsoring drug- and alcohol-free parties for graduating high-school seniors.

89

School-based drug-prevention programs teach students to resist peer pressure to use drugs and alcohol. In this classroom, students are role-playing how to "just say no" to a friend's offer of a can of beer.

Project Graduation celebrations usually include a parade for graduates and a "night to remember," which is guaranteed to be drug- and alcohol-free.[12]

Project STAR, another school program, teaches middle- and high-school students how to resist the pressure to try drugs. Homework assignments get parents involved in improving communication with their children and setting rules for acceptable behavior. Students involved with Project STAR showed reductions in smoking cigarettes, drinking alcohol, and taking illicit drugs.[13]

Communities and businesses also get involved in drug prevention. A few hundred people attended opening night at the Serendipity Cafe in Montclair, New Jersey. The cafe, a drug- and alcohol-free coffeehouse, features live entertainment and healthy snacks. High-school students came up with the idea for the cafe, which is in a formerly unused building in a local park. Local businesses donated tables and chairs, food, fruit juice, soda, and even flowers. Students help manage the cafe, from waiting on tables to performing onstage. The cafe gives young people an opportunity to get together at night away from the pressure to drink, smoke, and take drugs.[14]

Just Say No clubs are another way to spread the drug-free message to preteens and teens. The idea for the clubs came from former first lady Nancy Reagan. The clubs help young people learn to resist peer pressure to try drugs. They are in all fifty states and twelve foreign countries.

Alternatives to Drugs

One of the most important lessons to learn is that there are many positive alternatives to using drugs. Feeling good comes from within, through developing interests and learning new skills. Doing something you like, and doing it well, builds self-esteem and inner strength, producing a natural high.

There are many frightening stories and statistics about drug abuse. It is also important to remember, however, that millions of young people *do not* use drugs. There are positive alternatives to drug use. Some of these alternatives are:

- *competing in sports*
- *participating in scouting activities and after-school clubs*
- *playing a musical instrument*
- *working at a part-time job*
- *developing interests and hobbies: for example, photography, drawing, acting, dancing, or karate*

While LSD is not physically addictive, it can be psychologically addictive. Experts agree that the best way to avoid dependence on LSD is never to start. Taking LSD may seem like an exciting trip—but it is a trip to nowhere.

Questions for Discussion

1. When an LSD user is admitted to an emergency room, doctors are not required to report it to the police. Do you think this is a good idea? Why or why not?

2. It is very difficult for users to stop using drugs. Can you think of any encouraging words you could give to a friend who is trying to stay clean? What positive alternatives to drug use could you suggest to them?

3. High-school students in New Jersey started a drug-free coffeehouse in their town. What can you do in your community to help prevent or stop drug use?

Where to Go for Help

Many organizations offer help and information about drugs and drug use, treatment, and support for drug users, their families, and friends.

Information

American Council for Drug Education
136 E. 64th Street
New York, NY 10021
(212) 977-3354

D.A.R.E. America
P.O. Box 2090
Los Angeles, CA 90051-0090
(800) 223-DARE

Hazelden Foundation, Inc.
15245 Pleasant Valley Road, Box 11
Center City, MN 55012
(612) 257-4010

"Just Say No" International
2101 Webster Street
Suite 1300
Oakland, CA 94612
(800) 258-2766, (510) 451-6666

National Association on Drug Abuse Problems, Inc. (NADAP)
355 Lexington Avenue
New York, NY 10017
(212) 986-1170

National Clearinghouse for Alcohol and Drug Information
P.O. Box 2345
Rockville, MD 20847-2345
(800) 729-6686

National Families in Action Drug Information Center
2296 Henderson Mill Road #300
Atlanta, GA 30345
(770) 934-6364

Parent Resource Institute On Drug Education (PRIDE)
3610 DeKalb Technology Parkway, #105
Atlanta, GA 30340
(770) 458-9900

Parent to Parent PRIDE Parent Training
1240 Johnson Ferry Place, Suite F-10
Marietta, GA 30068
(800) 487-7743

Phoenix House Foundation

164 W. 74th Street
New York, NY 10023
(212) 595-5810

Treatment

(800) COCAINE

Operated by Phoenix House Foundation;
refers anyone with a substance abuse problem
to local counseling

Families Anonymous, Inc.

P.O. Box 3475
Culver City, CA 90231-3475
(800) 736-9805, (310) 313-5800

Narcotics Anonymous, Inc.

World Service Office
P.O. Box 9999
Van Nuys, CA 91409
(818) 773-9999

Chapter Notes

Chapter 1

1. Sidney Cohen, *The Beyond Within* (New York: Atheneum, 1964), p. 32.

2. Philippa Algeo, *Acid and Hallucinogens* (New York: Franklin Watts, 1990), p. 17.

3. Cohen, pp. 29–30.

4. A.J.S. Rayl, "LSD Psychotherapy," *Omni*, October 1992, p. 12.

5. Ibid., p. 12.

6. Evan Thomas, "Sins of a Paranoid Age," *Newsweek*, December 27, 1993, p. 20.

7. Martin A. Lee and Bruce Shlain, *Acid Dreams* (New York: Grove Weidenfeld, 1985), p. 296.

8. Jean Smith, "LSD: The False Illusion," *FDA Papers*, July–August 1967, pp. 15–16.

9. Ibid., p. 17.

10. Drug Enforcement Administration, *It Never Went Away—LSD, A Sixties Drug, Attracts Young Users in the Nineties* (Washington, D.C.: U.S. Department of Justice, p. 5.

11. Lloyd D. Johnston, Patrick M. O'Malley, and Jerald G. Bachman, *National Survey Results on Drug Use from The Monitoring The Future Study, 1975–1993* (Rockville, Md.: National Institute on Drug Abuse, 1994), vol. 1, p. 11.

12. Ibid., p. 201.

13. Neil Strauss, "The Acid Test," *Rolling Stone*, July 14–18, 1994, p. 24.

14. Lee and Shlain, pp. 180–182.

15. Strauss, p. 24.

16. Drug Enforcement Administration, *It Never Went Away—LSD, A Sixties Drug, Attracts Young Users in the Nineties* (Washington, D.C.: U.S. Department of Justice), p. 5.

17. Joe Mahoney, "It's a 60s Flashback: LSD Grows in Popularity," *Times Union* (Albany, N.Y.), May 18, 1994, p. A1.

18. Ibid.

19. Peter Wilkinson, "The Young and the Reckless," *Rolling Stone*, May 5, 1994, p. 29.

20. Ibid.

Chapter 2

1. Drug Enforcement Administration, *It Never Went Away—LSD, A Sixties Drug, Attracts Young Users in the Nineties* (Washington, D.C.: U.S. Department of Justice), p. 4.

2. Ibid., p. 3.

3. Joseph Treaster, "A New Generation Discovers Acid, and its Dangers," *The New York Times*, December 27, 1991, National Section, p. 15.

4. Drug Enforcement Administration, p. 3.

5. Jean Seligman, "The New Age of Aquarius," *Newsweek*, February 3, 1992, p. 67.

6. Mark Gold, "LSD: A Brief Profile," *Hallucinogens, LSD, and Raves* (symposium proceedings), (New York: American Council for Drug Education, 1993), p. 30.

7. Ibid., p. 31.

8. Richard Glennon, "How Do LSD and LSD-related Hallucinogens Work?," *Hallucinogens, LSD, and Raves* (symposium proceedings), (New York: American Council for Drug Education, 1993), p. 14.

9. Sharon Moeser, "Antelope Valley Teenage Intruder Under Influence of LSD Shot to Death by Homeowner," *Los Angeles Times*, April 12, 1994, metro section, p. 2.

10. Kenneth Kulig, "LSD," *Emergency Medicine Clinics of North America*, (August 1990), vol. 8, no. 3 p. 553.

11. Alison Bass, "Mentally Ill Patient in LSD Study Is Said to Have Killed Self," *Boston Globe*, January 5, 1994, metro section, p. 14.

12. Seligman, p. 67.

13. Gold, p. 33.

14. Substance Abuse and Mental Health Services Administration, *Tips for Teens About Hallucinogens* (Rockville, Md.: U.S. Department of Health and Human Services). Unpaged.

15. John O'Mahony, "Surf's Up For Beach Boy Brian Wilson," *New York Post*, August 15, 1995, p. 37.

16. Author interview with Special Agent Ronald Brogan and Assistant Special Agent in Charge Thomas F. Sheehan, Drug Enforcement Agency, Newark, N.J., January 27, 1995.

Chapter 3

1. Erich Goode, "Drug Abuse," *New Grolier Multimedia Encyclopedia* (Danbury, Conn.: Grolier Electronic Publishing, Inc., 1993), p. 4.

2. Susan and Daniel Cohen, *What You Can Believe About Drugs* (New York: Laurel Leaf Books, 1987), p. 107.

3. Goode, p. 4.

4. Mark Gold, "LSD: A Brief Profile," *Hallucinogens, LSD, and Raves* (symposium proceedings), (New York: American Council for Drug Education, 1993), p. 32.

5. Harry Shapiro, *Looking for the Man: The Story of Drugs and Popular Music* (New York: William Morrow & Co., Inc., 1989), p. 139.

6. Lloyd D. Johnston, Patrick M. O'Malley, and Jerald G. Bachman, *National Survey Results on Drug Use from The Monitoring The Future Study, 1975–1993* (Rockville, Md.: National Institute on Drug Abuse), vol. 1, p. 97.

7. Neil Strauss, "The Acid Test," *Rolling Stone,* July 14–28, 1994, p. 24.

8. Author interview with Robert Johnson, M.D., director, Adolescent and Young Adult Medicine, New Jersey Medical School, Newark, N.J., March 28, 1995.

9. *Toward a Drug-Free Generation: A Nation's Responsibility* (Washington, D.C.: National Commission on Drug-Free Schools, 1990), p. xi.

10. Johnston, O'Malley, and Bachman, pp. 23–24.

11. Michael Agar, "Hallucinogens: Who, What, When, Where, and Why?," *Hallucinogens, LSD, and Raves* (symposium proceedings), (New York: American Council for Drug Education, 1993), p. 5.

12. Author interview with Special Agent Ronald Brogan, Drug Enforcement Agency, Newark, N.J., Jan. 27, 1995.

13. David McDowell, "Ecstacy and Raves: The '90's Party Scene," *Hallucinogens, LSD, and Raves* (symposium proceedings), (New York: American Council for Drug Education, 1993), p. 12.

14. Ibid., p. 13.

15. Lillian M. Beard and Florence Isaacs, "Family Life in the '90's," *Good Housekeeping,* September 1993, p. 4.

16. Joan Goodman, "Case Histories of Adolescent LSD Users," *Hallucinogens, LSD, and Raves* (symposium proceedings), (New York: American Council for Drug Education, 1993), p. 37.

17. Author interview with Richard H. Schwartz, M.D., Newark, N.J., March 28, 1995.

18. Warren E. Leary, "Young People Who Try Suicide May Be Succeeding More Often," *The New York Times,* April 21, 1995, p. A15.

19. Richard H. Schwartz, George D. Comerci, and John E. Meeks, "LSD: Patterns of Use by Chemically Dependent Adolescents," *The Journal of Pediatrics,* December 1987, vol. 111, no. 6, part 1, p. 937; Phone interview, Richard H. Schwartz, M.D.

20. Peter Wilkinson, "The Young and the Reckless," *Rolling Stone,* May 5, 1994, p. 29.

21. Drug Enforcement Administration, *It Never Went Away—LSD, A Sixties Drug, Attracts Young Users in the Nineties* (Washington, D.C.: U.S. Department of Justice), p. 1.

22. Alison Landes, Nancy R. Jacobs, and Carol D. Foster, *Illegal Drugs and Alcohol: America's Anguish* (Wylie, Tex.: Information Plus, 1993), p. 121.

23. Holly Goodman, "Band's Fans Hit For LSD," *The Columbus Dispatch,* July 29, 1994, p. 2B.

24. Ibid.

Chapter 4

1. Phone interview with Joan Goodman, L.C.S.W., Rockville, Md., April 7, 1995.

2. Substance Abuse and Mental Health Services Administration, *National Household Survey on Drug Abuse: Population Estimates 1993* (Rockville, Md.: U.S. Department of Health and Human Services), October 1994, p. 47.

3. National Commission on Drug-Free Schools, *Toward a Drug-Free Generation: A Nation's Responsibility,* (Washington, DC), p. 7.

4. *Toward a Drug-Free Generation: A Nation's Responsibility* (Washington, D.C.: National Commission on Drug-Free Schools, 1990), p. 7.

5. Lloyd D. Johnston, Patrick M. O'Malley, and Jerald G. Bachman, *National Survey Results on Drug Use from The Monitoring The Future Study, 1975–1993* (Rockville, Md.: National Institute on Drug Abuse) vol. 1, p. 235.

6. Ibid., p. 41.

7. *Toward a Drug-Free Generation: A Nation's Responsibility*, p. 8.

8. Author interview with Special Agent Ronald Brogan, Drug Enforcement Agency, Newark, N.J., Jan. 27, 1995.

9. Ibid.

10. Substance Abuse and Mental Health Services Administration, p. 18.

11. Ibid., p. 47.

12. Ibid., pp. 48–49.

13. Ibid., p. 47.

14. Author interview with Stephanie Cooper (pseudonym), Rockleigh, N.J., April 12, 1995.

15. Johnston, O'Malley, and Bachman, p. 75.

16. Author interview with Stephanie Cooper.

17. Judy Monroe, *Alcohol* (Hillside, N.J.: Enslow Publishers, Inc., 1994) p. 54.

18. Phone interview with Richard H. Schwartz, M.D., Vienna, Va., March 28, 1995.

19. Author interview with Stephanie Cooper.

20. Phone interview with Bill Alden, deputy director, D.A.R.E., Los Angeles, Calif., June 5, 1995.

21. Author interview with Stephanie Cooper.

22. Ibid.

23. Phone interview with Joan Goodman, L.C.S.W., Washington, D.C., April 7, 1995.

24. Author interview with Stephanie Cooper.

25. *Toward A Drug-Free Generation: A Nation's Responsibility*, p. 14.

26. Phone interview with Joan Goodman.

27. Author interview with Stephanie Cooper.

28. Michael Agar, "Hallucinogens: Who, What, When, Where, and Why?," *Hallucinogens, LSD, and Raves* (symposium proceedings), (New York: American Council for Drug Education, 1993), p. 6.

29. Johnston, O'Malley, and Bachman, p. 274.

30. Author interview with Stephanie Cooper.

31. *Toward a Drug-Free Generation: A Nation's Responsibility*, p.14.

32. Author interview with Stephanie Cooper.

33. Phone interview with Robert Johnson, M.D., director of Adolescent and Young Adult Medicine, New Jersey Medical School, Newark, N.J., March 28, 1995.

34. Author interview with Assistant Special Agent Thomas F. Sheehan, Drug Enforcement Agency, Newark, N.J., Jan. 26, 1995.

35. Author interview with Stephanie Cooper.

36. Author interview with Bonnie C. Kauder, A.C.S.W., C.A.C., director of Adolescent Ambulatory Programs, Phoenix House Foundation, New York, May 8, 1995.

37. Richard H. Schwartz, George D. Comerci, and John E. Meeks, "LSD: Patterns of Use by Chemically Dependent Adolescents," *The Journal of Pediatrics*, December 1985, p. 936.

38. Author interview with Stephanie Cooper.

39. Schwartz, Comerci, and Meeks, p. 938.

40. Author interview with Bonnie C. Kauder.

41. Author interview with Stephanie Cooper.

Chapter 5

1. George Beschner and Alfred S. Friedman, *Teen Drug Use* (Lexington, Mass.: Lexington Books, D.C. Heath and Company, 1986), p. 196.

2. Author interview with Bonnie C. Kauder, A.C.S.W., C.A.C., director of Adolescent Ambulatory Programs, Phoenix House Foundation, New York, May 8, 1995.

3. Joan Goodman, "Case Histories of Adolescent LSD Users," *Hallucinogens, LSD, and Raves* (symposium proceedings), New York, American Council for Drug Education, 1993, p. 38.

4. Author interview with Bonnie C. Kauder.

5. Ibid.

6. Phone interview with Joan Goodman, L.C.S.W., Rockville, Md., April 7, 1995.

7. Beschner and Friedman, p. 13.

8. Author interview with Bonnie C. Kauder.

9. Al-Anon Family Group Headquarters, Inc., meeting table card, n.d.

10. *Parent to Parent Drug Prevention Workshop Outline*, Marietta, Ga., n.d.

Chapter 6

1. David Smith, "Haight Ashbury Revisited," *Hallucinogens, LSD, and Raves* (symposium proceedings), (New York: American Council for Drug Education, 1993), p. 52.

2. Kenneth Kulig, "LSD," *Emergency Medicine Clinics of North America*, August 1990, p. 555.

3. U.S. Department of Health and Human Services, *Annual Medical Examiner Data* (Rockville, Md.: Substance Abuse and Mental Health Services Administration, 1992), p. 25.

4. Smith, p. 52.

5. George Beschner and Alfred S. Friedman, *Teen Drug Use* (Lexington, Mass.: Lexington Books, 1986), p. 135.

6. Phone interview with Carl Prescott, Public Information Coordinator, Narcotics Anonymous, Van Nuys, Calif., May 30, 1995.

7. Gene R. Haislip, "Marketing the Product: The Buying and Selling of Ecstasy and LSD," *Hallucinogens, LSD, and Raves* (symposium proceedings), (New York: American Council for Drug Education, 1993), p. 48.

8. President George Bush, Statement from the White House, Washington, D.C., February 26, 1990.

9. Author interview with Bonnie C. Kauder, A.C.S.W., C.A.C., director of Adolescent Ambulatory Programs, Phoenix House Foundation, New York, May 8, 1995.

10. Author interview with Andrew O'Neill, Montclair, N.J., June 4, 1995.

11. Mary Ann Littell, "Hot Pursuit!," *Good Housekeeping,* March 1989, p. 60.

12. "Support MHS '95 Project Graduation," *Montclair Times,* June 15, 1995, p. A5.

13. *Toward a Drug-Free Generation: A Nation's Responsibility,* (Washington, D.C.: National Commission on Drug-Free Schools 1990), p. 49.

14. Katy McClure, "Recipe for Success: Serendipity and Faith," *Montclair Times,* June 15, 1995, p. 1.

Glossary

acid—Nickname for LSD.

acid lab—An illegal laboratory where LSD is manufactured.

blotter, blotter acid—Sheets of absorbent paper soaked in LSD solution and dried. The most common form of LSD available.

by-products—Chemicals that are left over when a substance is manufactured.

chemical warfare—The use of drugs and chemical substances as weapons of war.

compulsive—Uncontrollable, often used to describe drug use.

depression—Feeling unhappy or low.

detoxification—The removal of drugs and their effects from the body.

drug abuse—Nonmedical drug use that harms the user and others.

ergot—A fungus that grows on rye and other grains.

gangrene—The blackening and death of the body's soft tissues.

gateway drugs—Drugs that lead people to take stronger, more dangerous drugs.

generational forgetting—What happens when a new generation does not get the same chance as the previous generation to learn important messages.

hallucination—Seeing, hearing, or feeling things that are not real.

hallucinogens—A group of drugs that affect the central nervous system, producing a variety of vivid sensations and altering moods and thoughts. Some are artificial while others grow in nature.

high—The temporary feeling of relaxation and pleasure caused by taking certain drugs.

impulse—A message transmitted by a nerve cell or neuron.

ingest—To eat a substance.

intoxication—To stimulate or excite.

lysergic acid diethylamide—The chemical name for LSD.

medical addiction—Addiction to medicines.

metabolize—When the body breaks down a substance for use as fuel.

microgram—One-millionth of a gram.

microdot—Another common form of LSD; small tablets that are swallowed like pills.

multigenerational—Including many generations of people.

mucous membranes—The linings of the body passages and cavities.

narcotic—A drug that dulls the feeling of pain and produces a strong high.

neuron—The basic unit of the body's central nervous system.

neurotransmitters—Chemicals in the body that help nerve cells communicate.

palpitations—Rapid beating of the heart.

paranoia—When someone feels that everyone is out to harm him or her.

patent medicines—Medicines that were used to treat common ailments at the turn of the century.

polydrug user—Person who uses many different drugs.

prescription—A doctor's orders for a drug.

producing tolerance—When regular, repeated use of a drug causes it to lose its effects.

psychedelic—Generating hallucinations and distortions of perception. Also, a drug, such as LSD, that produces such effects.

psychoactive—A substance that influences or changes the way the mind works.

psychosis—A total loss of contact with reality, similar to a state of insanity.

rave—An all-night dance party where large quantities of drugs are available.

recreational drug use—Using drugs to get high.

relapse—To begin using drugs again after a period of not using them.

set limits—Establishing rules that others must follow.

synesthesia—The mixing of the senses; feeling sounds and hearing colors.

synthesize—To make a drug or other substance through a chemical process.

talk down—Talking calmly to reassure someone who is having a bad LSD trip.

trafficking—Dealing or selling drugs.

tranquilizer—A drug that calms and relaxes a person.

trip—The high a person experiences when on LSD.

windowpane—LSD in gelatin form that is made into small, thin sheets and cut in squares.

Further Reading

Algeo, Philippa. *Acid and Hallucinogens.* New York: Franklin Watts, 1990.

Campbell, Chris. *No Guarantees.* New York: New Discovery Books, 1993.

Cohen, Susan, and Daniel Cohen. *What You Can Believe About Drugs.* New York: Laurel Leaf Books, 1987.

Condon, Judith. *The Pressure to Take Drugs.* New York: Franklin Watts, 1990.

Currie, Cherie, and Neal Shusterman. *New Angel: The Cherie Currie Story.* Los Angeles: Price Stern Sloan, 1989.

Hurwitz, Sue, and Nancy Shniderman. *Drugs and Your Friends.* New York: Drug Abuse Prevention Library, 1992.

Knox, Jean McBee. *Drinking, Driving, and Drugs.* New York: Chelsea House, 1988.

McFarland, Rhoda. *Drugs and Your Parents.* New York: Drug Abuse Prevention Library, 1991.

Monroe, Judy. *The Facts About Stimulants and Hallucinogens.* Mankato, Minn.: Crestwood House, 1988.

Schwartz, Linda. *Drug Questions and Answers.* Santa Barbara, Calif.: Learning Works, 1989.

Seixas, Judith. *Living With A Parent Who Takes Drugs.* New York: Greenwillow Books, 1989.

Silverstein, Alvin, and Virginia Silverstein. *Addictions Handbook.* Hillside, N.J.: Enslow Publishers, 1991.

Stafford, Peter. *Psychedelics Encyclopedia.* Los Angeles: J. P. Tarcher, 1982.

Index

A

addiction, 36
Alcoholics Anonymous, 75
Army testing, 9
Aztecs, 8

B

bad trips, 12–13, 27, 28, 81
ban on LSD, 11
behavior changes, 68–69
blunts, 61
brain, effects on, 26

C

chemical warfare,
    testing for, 9
CIA, 9, 10
compulsive drug use, 45
Controlled Substances Act, 11, 46
cost of treatment, 85
crime, 61
crystal LSD, 20

D

DARE, 56, 88–89
DAWN (Drug Abuse Warning
    Network), 30
drop outs, 59
Drug Abuse Control
    Amendment of 1965, 11
Drug Enforcement Agency
    (DEA), 13, 32

E

early experiments, 9

early use, 6
Emory University, 9
emotional effects, 28
environment, 32
ergot, 5, 6
ethnic groups,
    treatment for, 85

F

Families Anonymous, 75
family counseling, 85
family life, 44
flaking, 61
flashbacks, 29, 63
Food, Drug, and
    Cosmetic Act, 9

G

gateway drugs, 40, 51
generational forgetting, 40

H

Haislip, Gene R., 87
hallucinations, 29, 63
hallucinogens, 12
health risks,
    long term, 31
Hofmann, Dr. Albert, 5, 6, 8
Holmes, Sherlock, 36

I

inpatient programs, 82
intervention, 71, 73
intoxication,
    acute, 81

J

Johnson, Dr. Robert, 61
Just Say No clubs, 91

L

laws,
    state and federal, 46, 48
Leary, Dr. Timothy, 15
lysergic acid, 5
lysergic acid diethylamide, 5

M

manufacturing, 20
medicine men, 8
metabolism, 24, 26
miracle tonics, 35

N

Nar-Anon World, 76
narcotics, 34
Narcotics Anonymous, 86
National Institute on Drug
    Abuse, 13
neuron, 26
neurotransmitters, 26

O

outpatient treatment programs,
    82–83, 84
overdoses, 30

P

Parent to Parent, 76
parental drug use, 66
patent medicines, 35
peyote, 8
polydrug use, 65–66
Project Graduation, 91
Project STAR, 91
pregnancy, 22
PRIDE, 76

Project Graduation, 91
Project STAR, 91
psychoactive drugs, 34, 35
psychological dependency, 24
psychosis, 29
Pure Food and Drug Act, 36

R

raves, 42–44
relapse, 86–87
residential treatment programs,
    83, 84
rock concerts, 15

S

Sandoz Pharmaceutical, 5–6
San Francisco, California, 19
school performance, 59
self-help groups, 74–77
sensory changes, 7–28
short-term crisis intervention, 82
siblings, 69
Sixties, 15, 16, 24, 37
St. Anthony's Fire, 7
stickers, 20, 22
suicide, 30, 45
Superman syndrome, 29

T

talking down, 81
tolerance, 22
treatment options, 79–80,
    82–85

U

user profile, 50, 52, 53

W

Wilson, Brian, 31
Woodstock generation, 37, 42